COMPUTE-IT
COMPUTING
FOR KS3

MARK DORLING
AND GEORGE ROUSE
Series Editors

Contributing authors:
James Abela
Ilia Avroutine
Phil Bagge
Mark Dorling
Graham Hastings
Sarah Lawrey
Zoe Ross
George Rouse
Genevieve Smith-Nunes
Carl Turland

Hachette UK's policy is to use papers that are natural, renewable and recyclable products and made from wood grown in sustainable forests. The logging and manufacturing processes are expected to conform to the environmental regulations of the country of origin.

Although every effort has been made to ensure that website addresses are correct at time of going to press, Hodder Education cannot be held responsible for the content of any website mentioned. It is sometimes possible to find a relocated web page by typing in the address of the home page for a website in the URL window of your browser.

Please contact Hachette UK Distribution, Hely Hutchinson Centre, Milton Road, Didcot, Oxfordshire, OX11 7HH. Telephone: +44 (0)1235 827827. Email education@hachette.co.uk Lines are open from 9 a.m. to 5 p.m., Monday to Friday. You can also order through our website: www.hoddereducation.co.uk

First published in 2014 by

Hodder Education
An Hachette UK Company,
Carmelite House,
50 Victoria Embankment,
London EC4Y 0DZ

Impression number   14
Year   2023

Cover photo © adimas – Fotolia

Typeset in ITC Veljovic Std by Phoenix Photosetting, Chatham, Kent.

Printed and bound by CPI Group (UK) Ltd, Croydon, CR0 4YY

A catalogue record for this title is available from the British Library.

ISBN 978 1 471 801921

Contents

Introduction iv

Unit 1   Under the hood of a computer 2

Unit 2   Think like a computer scientist 14

Unit 3   Drawing and manipulating shapes 30

Unit 4   Creating an animation 42

Unit 5   The foundations of computing 54

Unit 6   How the web works 66

Unit 7   Web page creation from the ground up 82

Unit 8   Designing for HCI: a hand-held digital device 98

Unit 9   Designing for HCI: an operating system interface 108

Unit 10   Representing images 116

Unit 11   Programming a calculator 130

Unit 12   Programming a quiz 140

Glossary/index 152

Acknowledgements 156

Introduction

Computing drives innovation in the sciences, in engineering, business, entertainment and education. It touches every aspect of our lives from the cars we drive to the movies we watch and the way in which businesses and governments communicate with and hear from us.

An understanding of Computer Science is essential if you want to keep up with changing technology and take advantage of the opportunities it offers in your life – whether it's as a career or a way of problem solving, or as a way of providing you with a greater appreciation of the way things work.

Computing is a relatively modern area of study but its roots go back to ancient times when our ancestors created calculating devices – long before modern-day calculators came into being. As you'll see, computer science also has a rich history of innovation and design.

While it is almost impossible to accurately predict what technological developments will happen next, there are underlying Computer Science concepts and principles that lead to future developments. These can be recognized and applied by people who work in computing.

Computational Thinking is one of these processes and it underpins all the learning in this Student Book. This should provide you with an approach to problem solving that you will be able to use in relation to a wide range of computer-related and non-computer related situations. By studying Computer Science you will develop valuable skills that will enable you to solve deep, multi-layered problems.

Throughout this Student's Book we have described the processes that led to the development of major ideas and systems. This will give you a much better understanding of how computing has come to be as it is today. We look at the development of computing through time, from ancient calculating devices to modern technology, highlighting how each break through or development has contributed to modern Computer Science. We look at the elements that make much of the technology we all take for granted today actually work, and we look at how you can apply this knowledge and these skills to computing challenges.

Each unit in the Student's Book centres around a challenge and, in order to gain the knowledge and skills you require to complete each challenge, you will come across three different types of activity:

- **Think-IT**: These are thinking and discussion activities to get you thinking about ideas and concepts.
- Plan-IT: These are planning exercises that set the scene for the practical activities.
- **Compute-IT**: These are the practical computing or 'doing' activities that will allow you to apply the skills and knowledge that you have developed within the unit.

We hope that you enjoy the challenges we have set you and your study of computing.

Mark Dorling and George Rouse

Challenge

Your challenge is to learn to 'think' like a computer, and understand how computers process data.

1.1 Under the hood of a computer

To compute

The word '**compute**' is derived from the Latin word 'computare', which means 'to count up', 'to sum up', 'to reckon together'. The Romans certainly did not have computers and 'to compute' does not mean to use a computer. Computing is something that we all do whenever we perform a mathematical calculation.

The electronic computer is not the first device that people have used to help them to compute. For many centuries mathematicians have been inventing tools to help them to carry out calculations with greater speed and accuracy.

▲ The first electronic computer, Colossus

▲ The Manchester Baby

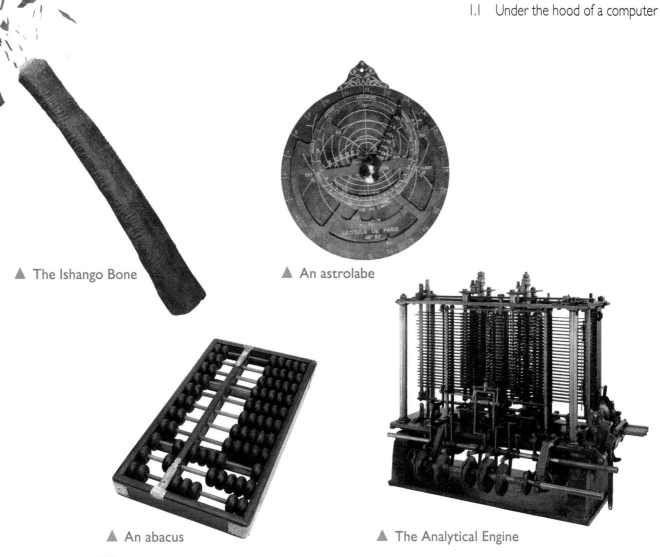

▲ The Ishango Bone

▲ An astrolabe

▲ An abacus

▲ The Analytical Engine

Think-IT

1.1.1   Draw a timeline stretching from the year 18 000 BC to today.

a) Where do the computing machines in the photographs fit on the timeline?

b) Can you think of any other computing devices or machines to add to the timeline?

Since prehistoric times and the very earliest civilisations there has been a need to compute in order to solve problems. The ancient Egyptians used mathematics to build their pyramids and the ancient Greeks applied geometry to their study of astronomy. Computing is so important that great mathematicians have always been highly revered. All over the world they have become well-known historical figures, such as the ancient Greek Pythagoras, Lui Hui from 3rd-century China, Muhammad Al-Khwarizmi from 9th-century Persia and Bhaskara from 12th-century India. You can find more details about famous mathematicians through time at **www.storyofmathematics.com/mathematicians.html**.

Think-IT

I.I.2   List all the computing devices you use at home and at school.

What is under the hood of a modern computer?

Traditionally we think of computers as the large desktop machines that many of us regularly use at home and at school. However, in recent years computers have become faster and smaller.

Compute-IT

I.I.3   **a)** Find an old computer to take apart. Make sure the machine is unplugged before you open the case and then examine all the component parts in turn. As you remove each part from the case, find out its function. Beware of sharp edges!

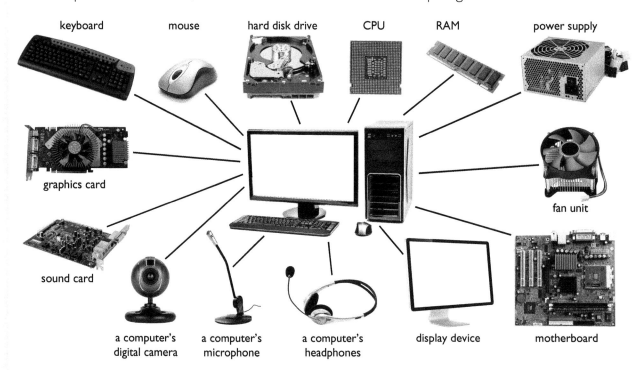

keyboard   mouse   hard disk drive   CPU   RAM   power supply

graphics card

fan unit

sound card

a computer's digital camera   a computer's microphone   a computer's headphones   display device   motherboard

▲ The main components of a computer

b) Now look at a Raspberry Pi, the credit-card-sized computer that you can plug into a TV and a keyboard. Can you locate the processor, the memory, the storage and the input and output?

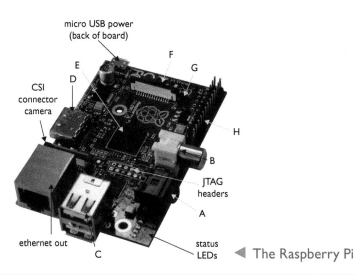

micro USB power (back of board)

F

E

D

G

CSI connector camera

H

B

JTAG headers

A

ethernet out

C

status LEDs

◀ The Raspberry Pi

It is possible to categorise the parts of a computer as **input devices**, **memory**, **storage devices**, **processor** and **output devices**.

Key Terms

Input device: An input device enables the user to 'input' data into a computer.

Memory: This is where a computer keeps the data that has been input, as well as software applications and the results of any processing it has carried out, for the short term. This memory is lost when the computer is off.

Storage device: This is where a computer stores files that have been created, as well as software that has been installed, for the longer term.

Processor: The part of a computer that processes data according to the instructions it has been given. It provides the user with information.

Output device: An output device enables the user to receive information from a computer.

Think-IT

1.1.4   Look at the table and name as many examples of each part of a computer as you can.

	Function	Examples
Input devices	Without external data a computer can do almost nothing. The role of the input device is to 'input' data into the computer.	
Memory	The computer has to keep the data that has been entered until it is ready to process it. It also has to load software applications. This memory is lost when the computer is off.	
Storage	Files and applications need to be stored safely until the computer is ready to load them again. This data is not lost when the computer is off.	
Processor	This is the part of the computer that processes data, according to the instructions it has been given, to provide the user with information.	
Output devices	Information has to be conveyed to the user. This function is performed by 'output' devices.	

Key Term

Central processing unit (CPU): The part of the computer that interprets and executes instructions.

Central Processing Unit

The **central processing unit** (the **CPU**) is sometimes described as the computer's brain. It is an important part of the computer system and it usually consists of a single integrated circuit (chip). It isn't as complicated as a human brain though. It thinks more like a function machine, which you might have come across in maths lessons.

▲ A central processing unit

The CPU has to be told what to do with the data. The instructions usually come from software applications, which are also known as 'computer programs'. In the illustration there are two instructions, 'multiply by 3' and 'add 7'.

The result of the processing, 19, is sent to an output device, usually a display, monitor or data projector, so that the user knows what it is. Note that the instructions have to be processed in the correct sequence, otherwise the result would be 33.

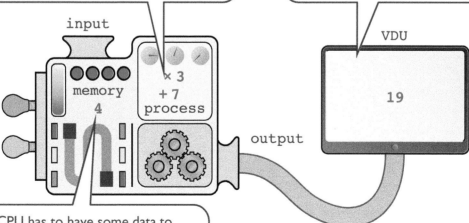

The CPU has to have some data to process. This is often input using a keyboard or a touch screen. The data is stored in the computer's memory. In the illustration the number '4' has been entered into the function machine's memory.

Think-IT

1.1.5   Which internal component of a computer can be regarded as a function machine in its own right?

Compute-IT

1.1.6   Create a function machine, like the one in the picture. Decide on an input, describe the processing that will take place and think about the resulting output. Now create three cards containing this information. Place the cards face down on the function machine. Turn over the input and output, and ask a fellow student to work out what the processing card has on it.

When a teacher asks you to do something, you listen (fetch), work out what you are being asked to do (decode) and then do it (execute). A CPU works in a similar way. It:

- fetches the instruction from memory.
- decodes the instruction to find out what processing to do.
- executes the instruction.

Think-IT

1.1.7   What have you learned about the CPU and what it can and cannot do?

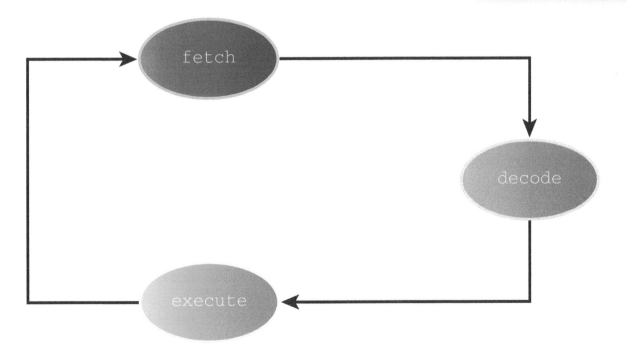

▲ A Fetch–Decode–Execute cycle

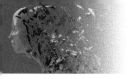
1.2 Code breakers

Enigma and the Lorenz machine

During the Second World War vital supplies were sent to Britain from the United States of America, but Nazi submarines (U-boats) were sinking large numbers of the ships bringing these supplies across the Atlantic. Winston Churchill understood that intelligence was crucial if Britain and its allies were to win the Second World War, and he put his faith in the team of code breakers at Bletchley Park. Their task was to decrypt Nazi communications. The Nazis were enciphering their messages using the Enigma machine and its successor, the Lorenz machine. If the Allies were able to break the codes, they could keep one step ahead of the Nazis.

▲ Some of the code-breaking team at Bletchley Park. Many of the code breakers were women.

▲ The Nazis used the Lorenz cipher machine to generate a code that they believed was unbreakable.

Colossus

Code breaking requires vast numbers of computations to be carried out extremely quickly. The team at Bletchley Park were working against the clock. Alan Turing, the mathematician who led the team, knew that humans were just too slow at performing the required volume of calculations, so the code breakers built a computer, known as Colossus (see the photograph on page 2), to speed things up. Colossus decrypted codes generated by the Lorenz Machine by carrying out complex analysis on the messages that were intercepted. Colossus could read 5000 characters per second. This meant that the analysis could be carried out in hours, rather than weeks. In a sense, Colossus was a function machine because it was programmed to perform just one task.

It took the enciphered input, processed it and, after many repetitions, produced the deciphered output.

A computer uses stored programs and must have writeable memory to store, load and run them. The Manchester Baby, developed shortly after the Second World War, was one of the first programmable computers. It was the ability to store and run programs that turned the special purpose computer, or function machine, into a general purpose computer.

The decimal number system

At school, you learn how to use the **decimal** number system, that is using units, tens, hundreds and thousands. The decimal number system is also known as base 10 because it uses ten different numbers – 0, 1, 2, 3, 4, 5, 6, 7, 8, and 9 – to make an infinite number of combinations.

Computers are electronic devices that use just two data values, 0 and 1. They can tell the difference between a high voltage and a low voltage, so we use high voltage to represent 1 and low voltage to represent 0. Using two values, 1 and 0, to represent numbers is known as **binary** or base 2. All data in a computer must be in binary, so anything that is to be processed or transferred between computers, including all words, sounds and images, must first be converted into a series of 1s and 0s.

Key Terms

Decimal: The system that is normally used for counting and computation. It uses ten digits: 0, 1, 2, 3, 4, 5, 6, 7, 8 and 9. The decimal number system is also called base 10.

Binary: A number system which uses two digits, 0 and 1. All electronic computation is carried out using the binary system. The binary number system is also called base 2.

Compute-IT

1.2.1   Think back to when you learned to organise numbers in multiples of ten, and then copy and complete the table.

Number	Hundreds	Tens	Units
146	1	4	6
	0	0	3
5			
24			
	0	6	5
93			
131			
	1	7	9
	2	1	3
255			

Circuit semaphore

Imagine an electric circuit with three lights, each controlled by its own switch. You can switch the lights on in many different patterns. Now imagine that each pattern represents a number, and each number relates to a message in a code book.

4   2   1

= 5

▲ Circuit semaphore

Think-IT

1.2.2 Look at the circuit semaphore diagram on the left. What do you notice about the number at the top of each column?

Compute-IT

1.2.3 **a)** Use the information contained in the circuit semaphore diagram on the left to work out what numbers the other four patterns of lights represent.

b) In the code book, the number 5 represents the question, 'What is your choice of meeting point, A, B or C?' The code book contains the following responses: 1 = A, 2 = B and 3 = C. What pattern of lights would an agent use to tell their controller to meet them at point B?

Binary

	LIGHTS		
	Left	**Middle**	**Right**
Decimal number	4	2	1
0	0	0	0
1	0	0	1
2	0	1	0
3	0	1	1
4	1	0	0
5	1	0	1
6	1	1	0
7	1	1	1

If you have three lights you can make the left-hand light represent '4', the middle light represent '2' and the right hand light represent '1'. A light can be 'on', represented by a '1', or 'off', represented by a '0'.

With just three lights, you can only represent the numbers 0 to 7, because '0' is 'all off' and '7' is 'all on'.

By switching on the light that equals '2', and switching off the lights that equal '4' and '1', you can display '2'.

By switching on the lights that equal '4' and '1', and switching off the light that equals '2', you can display '5'.

Compute-IT

1.2.4 **a)** Copy and extend the table below as required. Complete the cells for all the different binary combinations you can make. The first few cells have been completed for you.

1 bit	2 bits	3 bits	4 bits
0	00	000	
1	01	001	

Total number of 1 bit combinations:	Total number of 2 bit combinations:	Total number of 3 bit combinations:	Total number of 4 bit combinations:

b) You have seen how it is possible to count up to 7 in binary. How would you count to 8?

c) What is the largest number you can make with 1 bit? With 2 bits? With 3 bits? With 4 bits?

d) What is the smallest number you can make regardless of the number of bits?

e) What pattern can you spot when working out the largest number with a given number of bits?

f) What would you have to do if you wanted to count to 16?

g) What do you notice when you place a '0' to the right of a '1'?

Think-IT

1.2.5 In 1836, Samuel Morse, Joseph Henry and Alfred Vail invented a method of using electrical signals to send messages using a simple on/off system known as Morse code. The code is based on the length of time the circuit is switched on, and uses long and short signals to represent the letters in the alphabet. A short 'on' is called a dot and a long 'on' is a dash. For example, 'dot dot dot dash dash dash   dot dot dot' is the internationally recognised distress signal, SOS.

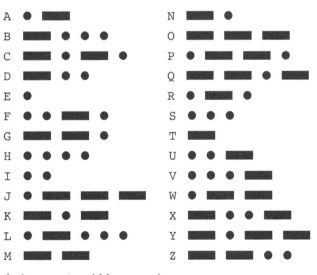

▲ International Morse code

Investigate other methods of sharing information through data transfer that have been used throughout history.

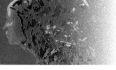

Bits and bytes

Computers use electrical circuits to process data. These circuits require the data to be in a digital form as a string of binary digits, or 1s and 0s. A bit is the name given to one binary digit and it is the smallest piece of data that a computer can process.

All the data stored on, and processed by, a computer is simply a long series of **bits**. To give an idea of scale, a single letter of text, for example the letter 'a', is represented by eight bits.

You have seen how a computer represents letters and numbers. Sound is digitised by sampling it at intervals, and images are digitised by representing coloured dots with binary numbers.

> **Key Term**
>
> **Bit**: The term 'bit' is used to describe one binary digit and is derived from **BI**nary digi**T**.

Kilobytes and megabytes

Many people generate computer files giving little thought to what these files consist of and how they are stored. The terms 'kilobyte' and 'megabyte' are used to describe the size of the storage space inside a computer; the amount of memory available to store data for use when processing and to store the output of the processing in the form of files. The prefix 'kilo' means thousand and 'mega' means million, so a 'megabyte' is one million **bytes**.

> **Key Term**
>
> **Byte**: A string of bits (usually eight, for example 10010101) is called a byte.

> A 'nibble' is half a 'byte'. Who says that computer scientists don't have a sense of humour?'

Unit	Size
Bit	A binary digit, 1 or 0
Nibble	4 bits
Byte	8 bits
kilobyte (kB)	1024 bytes
megabyte (MB)	1024 kB
gigabyte (GB)	1024 MB
terabyte (TB)	1024 GB
petabyte (PB)	1024 TB

▲ The common units for measuring digital data, computer file sizes and computer memory

Think-IT

1.2.6 Using your understanding of bits and bytes, convert the following values, which represent file sizes, into bits. Show your working.

a) 7 kB   **b)** 29 kB   **c)** 279 kB   **d)** 1 MB   **e)** 2 MB

1.2.7 The number 1024 keeps appearing. Where does this number come from?

From binary to information

In electronic computers all data items are processed in binary. Whatever form the input data takes, computers convert it into binary (into 1s and 0s) so it can be processed by a series of electronic switches within the CPU. The binary outputs are converted back into something that the user can easily understand, such as text and pictures.

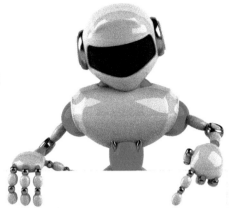

Challenge

Do you remember the challenge for this unit, to learn to 'think' like a computer, and understand how computers process data? Let's put your learning to the test.

Compute-IT

1.2.8 **a)** Create a plain text file. Type in the letters of the alphabet, then save the file as 'A'. Right click the file's name, select 'Properties' and record the size of the file in bytes and bits in a copy of the table below.

b) Why do you think file A has a size of 26 bytes?

c) How could you test your theory of why file A has 26 bytes?

d) Copy this sentence or one you make up yourself, which contains spaces and punctuation, into a text file and save it as 'B': 'The quick, brown fox jumps over the lazy dog. The lazy dog does not bark!' Now, copy and paste the sentence into a new text file twice and save it as 'C'. Finally, paste the sentence into a new text file five times and save it as 'D'. Complete the rest of the table below. What do you notice?

File	File type	Character count	Size (bytes)	Size (bits)
A: Plain text file (letters of the alphabet)	.txt	26		
B: Plain text file (sentence once)	.txt			
C: Plain text file (sentence twice)	.txt			
D: Plain text file (sentence five times)	.txt			

e) What is the size of one letter in bits?

Think-IT

1.2.9 How many average-sized reading books could be stored in a megabyte, assuming the files are not compressed?

Unit 2 Think like a computer scientist

Challenge

Your challenge is to create an emergency evacuation plan for your school.

2.1 Decomposition and algorithms

Decomposing a problem

Many of the things that you do every day you can probably do without thinking about them. It is only when you are asked to do something new that you really have to think. Imagine that you have been asked to teach a young child how to clean their teeth. On the face of it you probably think there is not much to it, but if the child is not able to clean their teeth properly this will lead to dental decay and possibly gum disease. Clearly you need to have a thorough understanding of what cleaning teeth really involves. You must **decompose** the problem. You must identify the actors and the actions and how the two work together to do the required task.

> **Key Term**
>
> **Decompose**: Break a problem down into a series of simpler problems, which you can easily understand. The process of decomposing a problem is known as 'decomposition'.

▲ A daily problem for you to solve

What is involved in brushing your teeth? What are the things you must do in order to make sure that your teeth are clean and your gums stay healthy?

- First, you need a brush.
- You also need some toothpaste.
- You have to start somewhere.
- You have to finish somewhere.

You have now decomposed the problem of how to brush your teeth. But is this enough? The first point in your list, 'First, you need a brush', raises some additional questions:

- What sort of brush do you need?
- You need a toothbrush, but should it be a manual or an electric toothbrush?
- If it is an electric toothbrush, is it charged up?
- If it needs charging, is there a suitable power point?
- If it is an electric toothbrush, do you have a brush head that fits?

These are questions you will return to.

Compute-IT

2.1.1 Think of a daily routine. It should be something that you can do without really thinking about it. Decompose the routine into as many simple steps as possible and write down each step. Nothing is too small or insignificant to include.

Here are some suggestions for routines you could decompose:

- Making a cup of tea
- Making a sandwich
- Feeding the cat
- Posting a letter
- Answering an email

When you have finished, swap your list of steps with a partner and challenge them to break your steps down into even smaller steps. Give them a point for every step they can decompose further. How many points did you each score?

Decomposing is a technique you can use to solve any problem. By decomposing it you will gain a much deeper understanding of the problem. You will also have broken your problem down into many simpler problems that are much easier to solve.

Writing an algorithm

Once you have decomposed a problem, the next stage is to list the sequence of steps you will need to follow to solve it. This is the process of writing an **algorithm**.

> ### Key Term
>
> **Algorithm**: A set of step-by-step instructions which, when followed solve a problem.
>
> The word algorithm is derived from the name of the Persian mathematician al-Khwarizmi.

◀ The Persian mathematician Muhammad al-Khwarizmi (AD 780–850)

Returning to the teeth-brushing problem, what might the algorithm look like? One way of planning an algorithm is to use a storyboard like this.

Problem/activity: **Brushing teeth**   *Alice Smith*

Step 1

> Find a brush

Step 2

> Add some toothpaste

Step 3

> Brush teeth

Step 4

> Rinse mouth

Step 5

> Put brush away

Step _____

>

▲ Alice's attempt at creating an algorithm for brushing teeth

Think-IT

2.1.2 Alice's algorithm isn't very good. She hasn't sufficiently decomposed the routine before writing it. Study her algorithm:

- Who or what are the actors and what are the actions?
- Can you see any patterns?
- Is it clear where you should start to brush and how much pressure you should apply when brushing your teeth?
- How do you know when to move from one tooth to the next?
- Do you know which direction to move the brush?
- How do you know when to finish brushing?
- Is the toothbrush put away at the end of the task?
- What else does your dentist tell you about brushing your teeth?

Compute-IT

2.1.3 Using an algorithm storyboard template, just like the one Alice used, rewrite her algorithm so that the instructions are clear, simple, detailed and precise. You will certainly need many more than five steps. When you have finished, swap your improved algorithm with your neighbour's and ask them to check that they can understand it and that nothing has been overlooked.

The process of decomposing a problem and writing an algorithm can be applied to solving much more complex problems. For example, it is a technique used by computer programmers when they develop software applications.

2.2 Data and pattern identification

Cholera in Soho

In 1854, the Soho district of London was being ravaged by cholera. Hundreds of people were already dead and more were dying every day. There did not seem to be anything anyone could do to stop the deaths. In those days germs had not yet been identified as the cause of cholera. A commonly held view was that it was 'miasma', foul smelling air, that spread the disease.

This was the challenge facing Dr John Snow. He did not accept the miasma theory and set about proving that something else was spreading cholera in Soho. Although the term was not used at the time, Snow applied some of the principles of **computational thinking** as he set about solving the problem and putting an end to the loss of life.

Identifying the problem

Dr Snow's first goal was to identify the problem. He began by gathering as much **data** and **information** as he could. An early breakthrough was his discovery that brewery workers rarely caught cholera. On further investigation he learned that brewery workers preferred to drink the free beer available to them instead of water. In decomposing the problem by asking the right questions, Dr Snow had hit upon a vital clue to the answer.

Think-IT

2.2.1 What do you think Dr Snow was able to deduce from this vital clue?

Identifying patterns

Dr Snow's next move was to focus on the cholera deaths to try to identify patterns in the data. To help him to do this he plotted the location of every cholera death on a map of the Soho area.

> **Key Term**
>
> **Computational thinking:** Thinking logically about problems (and the world) in terms of the processes involved, the data available, and the steps that need to be followed in order to achieve the desired goal.

> **Key Terms**
>
> **Data:** A collection of facts without context, such as values or measurements. For example, these numbers are data: 1 5 7 23 46 47 49.
>
> **Information:** Information is data that has been processed by adding a meaning through interpretation and by asking questions. For example, the data 1 5 7 23 46 47 and 49 become information when you know that they are lottery numbers. Data may also have different meanings in different contexts; 111 is one hundred and eleven in decimal, seven in binary, or could be interpreted as three letter Is (three in Roman numerals).

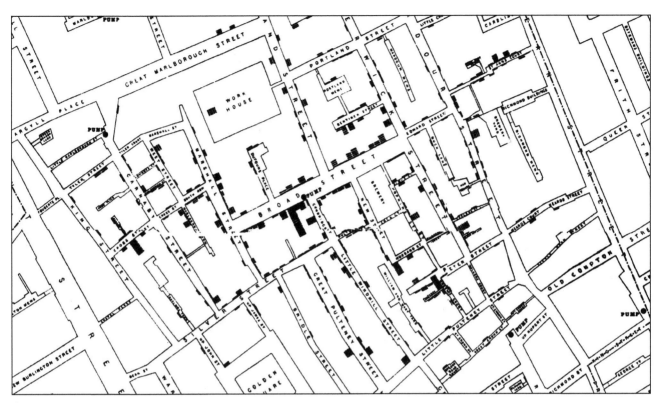

▲ Dr John Snow's original map of Soho in 1854. Note the black bars drawn on the map.
Each one represents the exact location of a death from cholera.

Compute-IT

2.2.2 Look at Dr Snow's map and, on a copy, carry out two important stages of computational thinking:

Collecting data

a) How many drinking water pumps are there in the Soho area?

b) Where are the pumps located? Mark them on your copy of the map.

c) Count the number of deaths in each street (each bar on the map represents a person who died of cholera). Record the number of deaths on the map.

Pattern identification and hypothesis testing

d) Colour code the streets where:

- more than 20 people died, in red
- between 16 and 19 people died, in orange
- between 10 and 15 people died, in yellow
- between 3 and 9 people died, in blue
- fewer than 3 people died, in green.

e) Once data has been processed it becomes information. So now look at the data you have processed and draw your conclusions. What do you think caused the Soho cholera outbreak and what would you do to prevent yet more people catching cholera?

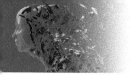

It is likely that you came to the same conclusion as Dr Snow. Well done if you identified the Broad Street pump as the cause of the outbreak. It turned out that a cesspit near the pump was leaking faeces into the pipes that supplied the pump, introducing cholera into the drinking water. Dr Snow acted quickly and had the handle of the pump removed so that it could not be used. As a result, no one else was infected by the water from the pump and the cholera epidemic soon died out.

Dr Snow's algorithm

It was John Snow's applied scientific method that helped to prove that there was something invisible in the water that infected people, and not foul smelling air. His genius was to gather the relevant data and analyse it correctly so that he could **model** the outbreak on his map and identify the centre of the infection. Dr Snow now had a life-saving algorithm:

1 Identify the problem.
2 Decompose the problem.
3 Collect data on location of deaths and on drinking water sources.
4 Perform **pattern identification** and **hypothesis testing**, comparing the distribution of deaths with the distribution of drinking water sources to identify the infected water source.

Dr Snow's solution to the 1854 cholera outbreak can be generalised. This means it can be applied to other outbreaks of cholera and to outbreaks of other diseases too. In fact, it is still being used today and has saved millions of lives.

Key Terms

Model: Something created to imitate a real-life situation.

Pattern identification: Looking for identifiable patterns in raw data using data analysis.

Hypothesis testing: A proposed explanation for something. You can test it, to see if it is correct, using scientific observation and investigation.

▲ Dr John Snow closed the Broad Street pump by removing the pump handle, and it remains without a handle to this day.

Malaria in Kitanga

Step I: Identify the problem

Malaria is the most deadly disease on Earth. It is spread by the *Anopheles* mosquito and kills millions of people every year. The most effective way of preventing malaria is to destroy the mosquito in its breeding grounds by spraying them with insecticide.

East African News

More deaths in Kitanga District

Over 600 people live in the four villages in Kitanga District in East Africa and recent deaths from malaria are causing great concern.

Village B, the largest village, with a population of 400, has already lost six people. Villages A and D both have populations of 100. So far only one person has died in Village A but three people have died in Village D in the last week. Village C has a small population of 30 people and, as yet, has not suffered any deaths.

The Anopheles *mosquito spreads malaria by biting people.*

Prompted by the deaths, a Government Health Minister visited Kitanga District and called for the immediate spraying of all the likely mosquito breeding grounds.

However, an association of village elders do not think mass spraying is the answer. 'Who will pay for the expensive chemicals?' they ask. They have also expressed concern about pollution. 'These are powerful chemicals. What effect will they have on the delicate ecosystem of the swamps which are an important source of fish as well as drinking water for our cattle?'

Use of mosquito nets, which prevent people from being bitten in the first place, is currently patchy. 50% of people in Village B use nets but this falls to 40% in Village D. Only 20% of people use nets in Village A and only 10% use them in Village C.

The local Kitanga clinic has just published the infection rates for the four villages in the district:

Village	Number of people infected	Number of deaths
A	1	1
B	14	6
C	3	0
D	9	3

Think-IT

2.2.3 What would you do to put a stop to the outbreak?

Two very important aspects of computational thinking are the ability to solve a problem systematically and to generalise once an algorithm has been formulated. **Abstraction** and **generalisation** are used to apply an algorithm to different problems that have similar features. Learning from Dr Snow's success in Soho in the nineteenth century, it is possible to apply generalisation to this particular twentieth-century problem of the malaria outbreak in Kitanga. You have already identified the problem, which is Step 1 of Dr Snow's algorithm, so now it is time to move on to Step 2.

Step 2: Decompose the problem

What are the questions you need to ask to understand the problem facing the village elders? This is a problem that is already well understood. You know that malaria is transmitted by a parasite carried by the *Anopheles* mosquito. Humans are infected when they are bitten by a mosquito carrying the parasite. You also know that the preferred breeding ground for mosquitoes is stagnant water such as swamps.

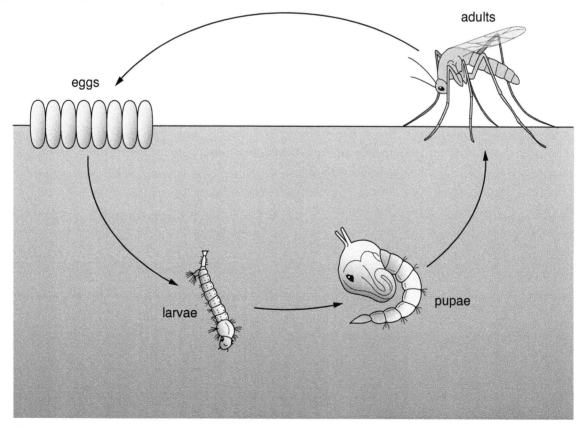

▲ The life cycle of a mosquito

Step 3: Collect data

The newspaper article and a map of Kitanga District can supply you with a lot of useful data. You need to extract as much information as you can from the data, so you can analyse it thoroughly and look for any patterns.

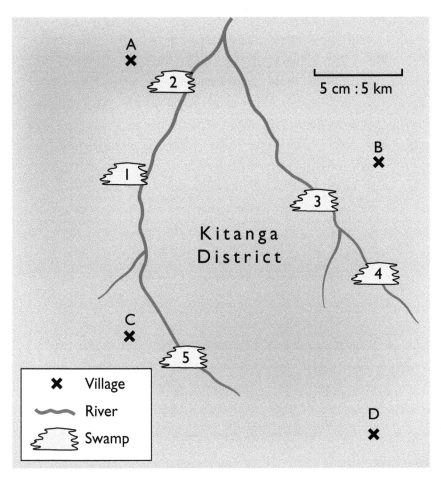

▲ Kitanga District of East Africa

Compute-IT

2.2.4 Create a spreadsheet to organise the data you have collected.

Step 4: Perform pattern identification and hypothesis testing

A model is something that people create to imitate a real-life situation and help them analyse data. Computers are often used for modelling, particularly where numerical data is concerned. A spreadsheet can quickly and accurately carry out all the complicated calculations needed to produce a computer model and display the results in a graph to make it easier to spot patterns.

A computer can do in seconds what it would take a human many months or, in some cases, years to do.

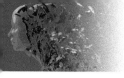

Compute-IT

2.2.5 Use the spreadsheet containing the data you have collected to create three models in the form of three graphs:

- Model 1: The number of people infected by the swamp nearest to them.
- Model 2: The percentage of the population of each village infected by the swamp nearest to them, because each village has a different population and you need to compare like with like.
- Model 3: The percentage of the population of each village who do not use mosquito nets and who were infected by the swamp nearest to them.

Think-IT

2.2.6 Examine the graphs you have created. Which swamp should be sprayed?

Each of the three models points to a different swamp as the source of the outbreak of malaria in Kitanga.

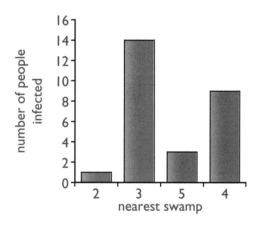

◀ Model 1: A simple model based on the number of people infected points to Swamp 3 as the cause of the outbreak

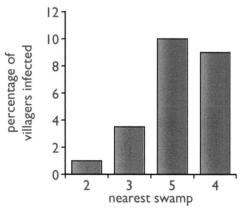

▲ Model 2: When you consider the percentage of villagers infected, the data points to Swamp 5 as the cause of the outbreak

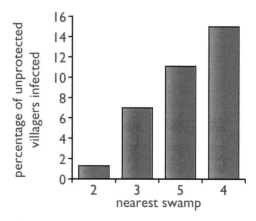

▲ Model 3: If you remove the protected population from the data it tells you that Swamp 4 is the one to spray with insecticide

Think-IT

2.2.7 An important aspect of computational thinking is to be able to evaluate solutions and identify the best one.

a) Consider which of the three models is the most efficient. Which one requires the least amount of data entry?

b) Does the most efficient model provide the most effective algorithm for identifying the cause of the outbreak?

c) Compare and contrast the three solutions and rank them in order, providing reasons for their rankings.

Remember, although a model is a useful tool, it is only an imitation of real life and, in fact, it is possible that more than one swamp is infected. If that is the case you might need a more complex model to solve this problem.

Step 5: Create an algorithm

Compute-IT

2.2.8 Write an algorithm that can be used by village elders in the future or by elders in other districts to help them to eliminate future outbreaks of malaria. You could use an algorithm storyboard template to help you.

Remember, your algorithm should not be specific to Kitanga District, but must be abstracted and generalised to be useful to any district in East Africa.

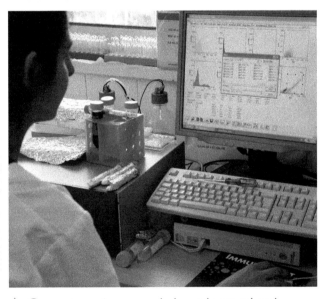

▲ Computer science can help understand and prevent many serious diseases like malaria around the world

2.3 Emergency evacuation

Challenge

We all take evacuation plans for granted. How many people actually listen to the flight attendants when they give the safety talk just before an aeroplane takes off? A good evacuation plan can be a real life-saver and your challenge is to draw up a new emergency evacuation plan for your school.

Create a new emergency evacuation plan and map, which explains how people should leave the building and move as quickly and as safely as possible to an assembly point. The plan must also include a way of checking that everyone has arrived safely at the assembly point.

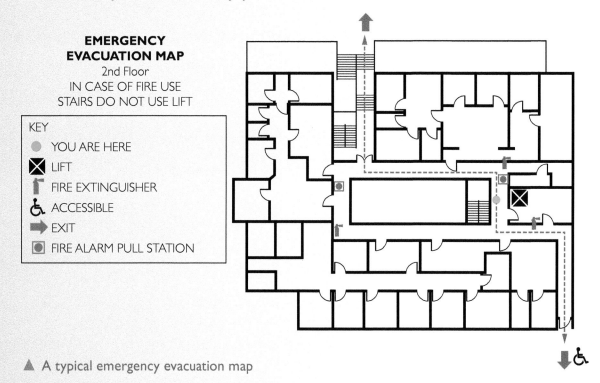

EMERGENCY EVACUATION MAP
2nd Floor
IN CASE OF FIRE USE
STAIRS DO NOT USE LIFT

KEY
● YOU ARE HERE
✖ LIFT
▐ FIRE EXTINGUISHER
♿ ACCESSIBLE
➡ EXIT
◉ FIRE ALARM PULL STATION

▲ A typical emergency evacuation map

You will need to use computational thinking to complete the challenge.

Compute-IT

2.3.1 Identify the problem

Writing an evacuation plan for the whole school is an enormous task, so begin by defining the scope of your plan. What is the exact part of the school your plan is going to cover? It might be a whole block, a whole floor or a single classroom.

Compute-IT

2.3.2 **Decompose the problem**, breaking it down into a number of smaller problems. For instance, you could decompose the building into floors and stairs; the floors into rooms and corridors; and the rooms into doors, aisles and desks. Here are some suggestions for questions you could ask yourself to help you decompose the problem:

- Visualise the problem: Imagine an emergency evacuation. What is likely to happen?
- How many people might be in the building? You could decompose the actors into teachers and students.
- What are the possible routes out of the building? Start with a student at a desk, and decompose their actions into desk → aisle; aisle → door; door → corridor; corridor → stairs, and so on.

- Which is the best route out of the building? Is it the shortest route or the quickest route? How should you measure 'best'?
- What data do I need?
- What data is available?
- How can I collect more data?
- Where should people assemble?
- Do I need to cater for anyone with special needs?
- How will I know if everybody is safe?

Compute-IT

2.3.3   **Collect data**

Your plan must be based on accurate data, which you will need to collect. It is no use estimating the length of a corridor or guessing how long it might take a child to walk down a flight of stairs. Ideally you should walk the possible evacuation routes, measuring widths of corridors and doorways, measuring distances, counting stairs and identifying possible hazards and obstructions. You should test and time possible evacuation routes so that you can base your solution on real data. You will also need to calculate the maximum number of people to be evacuated.

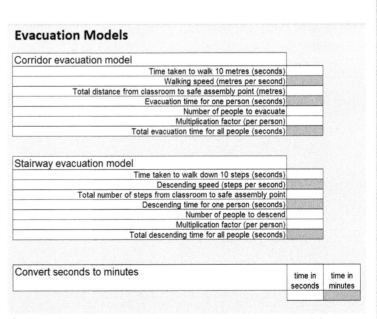

▲ Data handling could be carried out using a spreadsheet.

Compute-IT

2.3.4 Pattern identification and hypothesis testing

Use a spreadsheet to record your data and to carry out analysis and modelling.

The data for the first floor of a block will be the same as for the second and third, but with additional time for each staircase. If you have calculated the time for one student to descend a flight of stairs safely, can you add a multiplication factor to allow you to model different numbers of students? A plan that works well when only one class is in the block might be a disaster if there are five classes. Where are the bottlenecks that will slow down the evacuation? Do you need more than one evacuation route?

- Are there any patterns in the data that will help you create an efficient solution to the problem? For instance, instead of repeating instructions again and again in the same words, can you refer to previous instructions instead?
- Are corridors the same length and width?
- Are all the stairwells the same size with the same numbers of stairs?
- If you are evacuating a three-story block, does each floor have the same floor plan? Can the same instructions be applied to each floor?

Compute-IT

2.3.5 Abstraction

As you think about creating your evacuation plan and map, try not to think of the whole solution from beginning to end. Instead, tackle each aspect of the evacuation process separately. Make sure that each small stage in the process works perfectly before you move on to the next stage. Lining people up at an assembly point or carrying out a roll call are, for example, very different processes from moving people out of a classroom or down a stairwell.

▲ How will you check that everyone is out of the building?

Compute-IT

2.3.6 Write the algorithm that will serve as your evacuation plan. Like all good algorithms, your instructions must be:

- clear
- unambiguous
- precise
- correctly sequenced.

Your evacuation plan should be designed as a poster, which includes a set of instructions and possibly a diagram, for the classroom wall.

Think-IT

2.3.7 If you were asked to write an evacuation plan for a different part of your school, would you have to start from the beginning again? Are there aspects of your plan that could be reused by applying them to a different but similar problem? If there are, this is generalisation at work.

▲ How far can you generalise? Would your plan work for a different school? Would it work for a Victorian school and a modern school? Could you expand your plan for a larger building such as a hotel or a hospital? How much of your solution could be applied to a railway station or a cruise ship?

Unit 3 Drawing and manipulating shapes

Challenge

Your challenge is to write a program that creates an artwork based on drawing and positioning shapes found in Celtic or Islamic art.

3.1 Shapes, patterns and algorithms

Computer science, art and maths

There are many ways in which computer science is linked to the world around us and there are very strong links between maths, art and computer science.

The term **abstraction** can be used in all three subjects. In computer science abstraction means finding **generalisations** by identifying common patterns in real situations.

In maths, abstraction involves considering a problem theoretically, separating it from the everyday contexts that it has been associated with in the past, so that generalisations can be used in other contexts. Abstraction, in art, describes the process of interpreting the subject rather than depicting it exactly.

Being creative and imaginative are skills that artists and computer scientists need. Just think of the creativity that goes into designing the video games you play. The characters, environments, graphics and game-play are all developed by designers and programmers working together.

Mathematicians, artists and computer scientists all need to solve problems and find patterns in their work. For example, when trying to find a cure for a disease, scientists will look for patterns in the medical data of people who are already ill with the disease.

Key Terms

Abstraction: Working with ideas or solving a problem by identifying common patterns in real situations, concentrating on general ideas and not on the detail of the problem itself.

Generalisation: Taking concepts used in the solution of a particular problem and using them to solve other problems that have similar features.

(You used both abstraction and generalisation when you tackled the problem of the malaria outbreak in Kitanga District in Unit 2.)

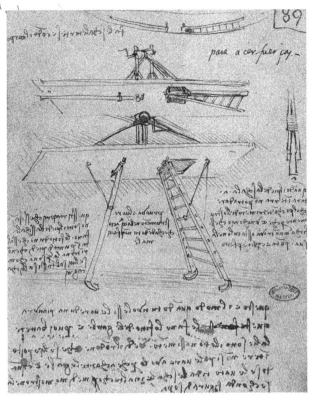

▲ Leonardo da Vinci was an artist, scientist, mathematician and inventor. He would probably have been a great computer scientist too, had modern technology existed during his lifetime. He was an abstract thinker and would often take ideas from one area, identify the important concepts and apply these to another area. He was applying computational thinking skills to problem solving.

Think-IT

3.1.1 In what other ways do you think computer science, art and maths are linked? The images below should provide some food for thought.

▲ The original plans for the London 2012 Olympic and Paralympic Stadium and a photograph of the finished stadium

Shapes

Shapes, and **geometrical shapes** in particular, play an important part in maths, art and computer science.

A square is a geometrical shape. The key features of a square are:

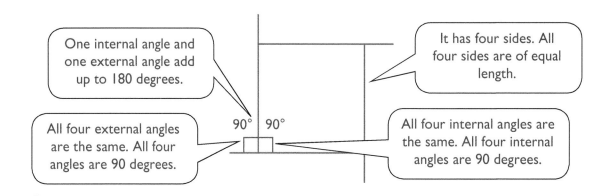

One internal angle and one external angle add up to 180 degrees.

It has four sides. All four sides are of equal length.

All four external angles are the same. All four angles are 90 degrees.

All four internal angles are the same. All four internal angles are 90 degrees.

$90°$ $90°$

Think-IT

3.1.2   What shapes can you see around you? Look at the objects below. Redraw them as shapes and label their features.

a

b

c

d

Patterns

Patterns also play an important part in our lives. Patterns are repeated concepts defined by rules. From number patterns to visual and scientific patterns, they are everywhere! Patterns help us to see and understand how things work.

Think-IT

3.1.3 **a)** What patterns can you recognise in these number sequences?

11, 22, 33, 44   2, 4, 8, 16

b) What are the next three values in each series?

c) What patterns can you recognise in photographs b, c and d on page 32?

d) Look around you. What repeating patterns can you see?

Algorithms

Theo van Doesburg was an abstract artist. He often explored the shape and colour of objects by representing them as geometric shapes.

Think-IT

3.1.4 What shapes can you see in van Doesburg's painting?

Van Doesburg's paintings are made up of squares, rectangles and lines of different sizes. By looking at the painting in this way, you have undertaken **decomposition**.

Decomposition is used to solve problems by breaking them into smaller parts. For example, if you want to make a packed lunch for school, you will naturally break the task down into smaller parts, making sandwiches, making a drink and adding your other favourite lunch foods. To solve the problem of creating a van Doesburg-style artwork, the challenge is how to create the squares, rectangles and lines that make up one of van Doesburg's paintings. Let's start with drawing a square.

Key Term

Decomposition: The process of breaking something down into smaller parts.

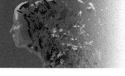

Key Term

Algorithm: A set of step-by-step instructions which, when followed, solve a problem.

Designing an algorithm

An **algorithm** is a set of step-by-step instructions which, when followed, solve a problem. We can use an algorithm to help us draw our square.

 **Plan-IT**

3.1.5 a) Imagine you have to give an alien instructions on how to draw a square. What would you tell the alien to do? Write down your instructions and give them to a friend to try out.

HINT: Use the following as a starting point. Can you improve on these instructions?

- Put your pen on the centre of a piece of paper.
- Draw a 5 cm line straight up the page.
- Turn the pen 90 degrees to the right.

b) Did your friend manage to draw a square? Do you need to adjust your instructions?

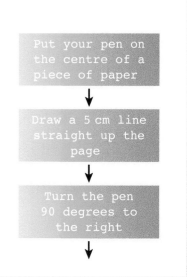

Put your pen on the centre of a piece of paper

↓

Draw a 5 cm line straight up the page

↓

Turn the pen 90 degrees to the right

↓

Refining an algorithm

Van Doesburg's paintings have lots of shapes in different places. Each shape has a different location on the canvas, but how do we specify that location?

Mathematicians use **coordinates** to identify a specific location by giving two values:

- x tells you where the location is horizontally
- y tell you where the location is vertically.

A computer understands coordinates, so it is possible to tell a computer where to start drawing a shape using x and y values to specify the starting point.

Key Term

Coordinates: A set of values used to show an exact position. In two dimensions we use x and y values, where x is the distance across the page and y the distance up the page.

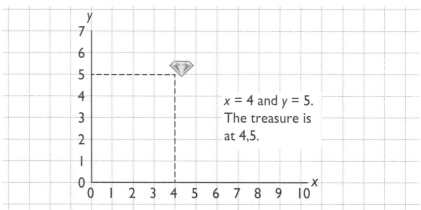

$x = 4$ and $y = 5$. The treasure is at 4,5.

Plan-IT

3.1.6 Plot an *x* axis and a *y* axis on piece of squared paper. Number each axis from 0 to 20. Draw three squares in different locations and in different colours on the grid.

Write an algorithm for your alien telling it how to draw the squares. How are you going to tell it what colour to use for each square and when to pick up and put down the pen?

Making algorithms efficient

It is important that algorithms are as efficient as possible. Making an algorithm short and expressing it clearly helps us to describe the pattern of repeated actions more effectively. One of the ways you can make an algorithm shorter is to repeat instructions; to use **iteration**. Look at the two examples of an algorithm on the right. The algorithms are basically the same, but the second one is shorter because we say repeat the left right pattern five times rather than writing it all out five times.

```
Without iteration

Put right foot forward
Put left foot forward
Put right foot forward
Put left foot forward
Put right foot forward
Put left foot forward
Put right foot forward
Put left foot forward
Put right foot forward
Put left foot forward
```

```
With iteration

Repeat the following
  five times:
Put right foot forward
Put left foot forward
```

> **Key Term**
>
> **Iteration:** Using repetition of a process to create a more efficient solution.

Plan-IT

3.1.7 Look at the instructions for drawing three squares that you wrote for 3.1.6 Plan-IT. Can you use iteration to make your algorithm shorter and clearer?

3.1.8 To draw a square you need to turn through 90 degrees each time you need to turn a corner. This is the external angle.

a) What are the external angles – the angles you must turn through when drawing the shape – for:

- a regular triangle
- a regular pentagon
- a regular hexagon
- a rectangle?

b) What would a shape with 360 sides look like?

c) Write an algorithm for drawing a triangle, a rectangle, a pentagon and a hexagon.

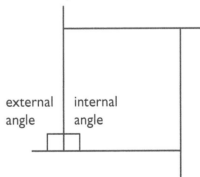

external angle   internal angle

3.1.9 On paper draw your own van Doesburg-style artwork, based on geometric shapes. Later, you will be creating algorithms to enable a computer to draw your design, so think about the shapes, patterns and colours you use and where they will appear on the page. For example, will you use squares, rectangles and lines like van Doesburg or will you include other shapes in your design? Will you stick to bold, primary colours, or introduce other colours into your artwork? You can be as creative as you like!

3.2 Drawing and manipulating shapes using graphical programming software

▲ Paired programming in action

Unit 3.1 explored van Doesburg's artwork and how to create an algorithm for drawing a square using iteration. Now we are going to find out how to use graphical programming software to create geometrical shapes. We can use decomposition and abstraction to do this.

Paired programming

'Paired programming' is a term used in industry to describe a method of programming where two programmers work together on one computer. One programmer – the driver – writes the code, while the other – the observer – reviews each line of code (the technical name for the instructions given to the computer) and debugs it (the name given to the process of correcting code), developing ideas and generally looking for improvements.

Plan-IT

3.2.1 a) In 3.1.9 Plan-IT you drew your own van Doesburg-style artwork. Now, list the geometrical shapes in your drawing.

   b) Using paired programming, write an algorithm for each geometrical shape. For example:

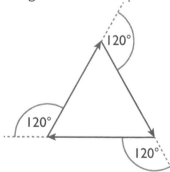

1. Choose red pen
2. Place pen in location (5,10).
3. Draw a 5 cm line horizontally from right to left.
4. Turn the pen 120 degrees to the left.
5. Repeat steps 3 and 4 three times.

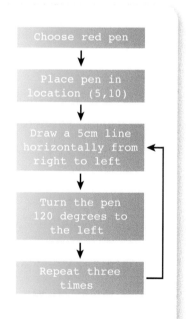

From algorithm to graphical programming

A computer will not be able to understand the plain English algorithms you have written. It needs you to program in a way that 'translates' your algorithms into a language it can understand. You can do this using graphical or text-based programming software.

Graphical programming represents elements visually rather than textually, often using graphics in a drag-and-drop interface. Graphical programming software is a good place to start learning how to program, before moving on to writing programs with a text-based programming language.

Key Term

Graphical programming: A programming language that allows users to create programs using graphics rather than text.

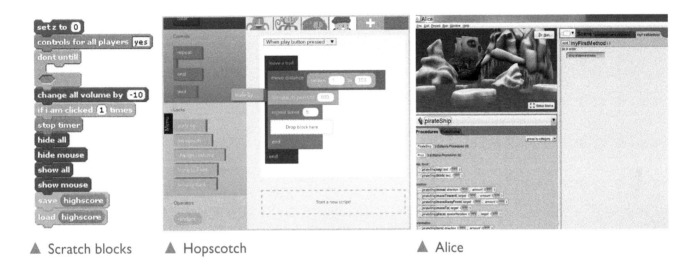

▲ Scratch blocks   ▲ Hopscotch   ▲ Alice

Compute-IT

3.2.2 a) Using paired programming, convert the algorithms you have created into your chosen graphical programming language.

HINT: Have you remembered to use iteration to ensure your algorithm is as efficient as possible to write?

In Scratch, this can be done by using the 'Repeat' block, which you can use to specify how many times an instruction should be repeated.

b) Write a program that will position the shapes automatically to create a short animation.

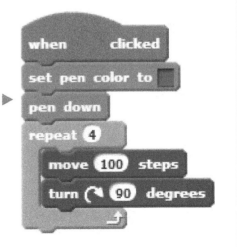

3.3 Drawing and manipulating shapes using text-based programming software

Celtic and Islamic art

Celtic art and Islamic art use patterns and shapes to represent the natural world in an abstract way.

Examples of Islamic and Celtic objects. In the Islamic object above, the design is created from a series of overlapping regular dodecahedrons (12-sided shapes). In the Celtic object, on the left, the shapes are more curved with circles and loops.

Think-IT

3.3.1   Both Celtic and Islamic art make use of pattern and shape, but in a very different way to van Doesburg. What similarities and differences can you see between the two different artworks below and the van Doesburg painting on page 33? Consider the shapes used and the way they are positioned.

▲ An example of Celtic art   ▲ An example of Islamic art

Text-based programming languages

Text-based programming requires the user to write code in the form of a sequence of text-based instructions into the computer to create a program. The program controls a 'turtle', or cursor, on the screen.

Text-based programming languages are used to create programs that perform many different tasks. Most of the interactivity you experience on websites and mobile apps is created using text-based programming languages such as these:

> **Key Term**
>
> **Text-based Programming:**
> A programming language that requires the user to write code in the form of a sequence of text-based instructions into the computer to create a program.

▲ Python   ▲ C++   ▲ Ruby

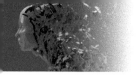
Writing a program to draw shapes using a text-based programming language

If you already know how to create a program to draw geometrical shapes using a graphical programming language, it will help you to do the same thing using a text-based programming language.

Think-IT

3.3.2 Look at the two sets of instructions below, and match the graphical instructions to the text-based instructions.

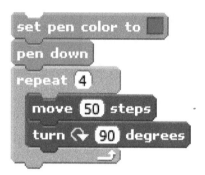

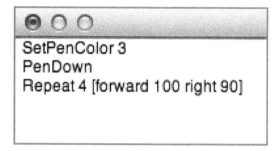

```
SetPenColor 3
PenDown
Repeat 4 [forward 100 right 90]
```

The graphical programming software used in the example is Scratch and the text-based programming language is Logo.

Plan-IT

3.3.3 Write algorithms for each of the following shapes:

- A red square
- A yellow triangle
- A green pentagon
- A shape of your choice

Most programming languages allow you to use iteration to clarify the processes being used. For example, we can create a new instruction to draw a square and name it 'square'. We can then re-use that instruction elsewhere in our program.

In Logo we can define the instruction 'square' as follows:

```
to square
repeat 4 [forward 50 right 90]
end
```

We can now use the instruction 'square' more than once in our program. For example:

```
repeat 36 [right 10 square]
```

Compute-IT

3.3.4 Using a text-based programming language, enter the code required to draw the shapes you wrote algorithms for in 3.3.3 Plan-IT.

Challenge

Do you remember the challenge at the beginning of the unit, to create an artwork based on drawing and positioning shapes found in Celtic or Islamic art?

Plan-IT

3.3.5 a) Design an artwork based on drawing and positioning shapes found in Celtic or Islamic art.

b) Create an algorithm for your artwork. Use paired programming, as well as abstraction, decomposition and iteration.

Compute-IT

3.3.6 Using a text-based programming language, enter the code required to draw your artwork.

Challenge

Your challenge is to program an animation to entertain an audience by recreating a dance routine from a music video using programming techniques such as sequences, iteration, procedures, selection and variables.

4.1 Algorithms

How important is an accurate algorithm?

As you discovered in Unit 3, an **algorithm** is a set of step-by-step instructions which, when followed, solve a problem. A dance routine, at a very basic level, is a set of set-by-step instructions given to a dancer. A parallel can therefore be drawn between an algorithm and a dance routine, and an algorithm should form the starting point for solving the challenge.

> ### Key Term
>
> **Algorithm**: A set of step-by-step instructions which, when followed, solve a problem.

Compute-IT

4.1.1 Watch 20 to 30 seconds of a dance video and list the dance moves you see. You could describe each move as part of a flowchart or you could draw stick people as part of a storyboard to illustrate them.

Algorithms have to be accurate to be effective. You learnt in Unit 3 that an inaccurate algorithm produces poor results when drawing shapes, just like a dancer with inaccurate instructions produces a very poor dance routine. It is therefore important to think carefully about each step in the process and how they are linked together. Running through exactly what the algorithm says, step-by-step, is called a **dry run** and it will help to make the final algorithm more accurate.

> ### Key Term
>
> **Dry run**: To run through a program on paper to see how it works. A dry run records the state of each variable when each line of the program is executed, so it has one line for each line of code in the program.

Think-IT

4.1.2

a) What would happen if a troupe of dancers didn't follow their dance routine algorithm accurately? How would you know if a dancer made a mistake during a dance routine?

b) What sort of inaccuracies in the algorithm itself could cause a poor result, a poor dance routine?

c) What would need to happen if one of the dancers had a solo during the dance routine?

Robots **execute** programs based on algorithms, just like a dancer executes a sequence of moves in time to music.

Key Term

Execute: To carry out something, usually a set of instructions.

Compute-IT

4.1.3 In pairs, decide who is going to be a robotic arm and who is going to provide the instructions to control it. The instruction provider must tell the arm what to do to pick up an object, such as a pencil, and move it from one location to another specified location, and must write down the instructions as they provide them. The robotic arm should close their eyes and use their arm and hand to follow the instructions given to them.

▲ It is important for a robot to perform its tasks accurately when assembling a car, for example.

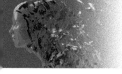

Think-IT

4.1.4 Think about 4.1.3 Compute-IT.

   a) What difficulties did you face when you gave and received instructions? How could you remove these difficulties?

   b) The instructions the instruction provider gave to the robotic arm were an algorithm. Did you notice how the algorithm contained lots of opposites? Why do you think this is the case?

   c) Can your algorithm be used again?

   d) What would you have to do to reuse the algorithm created for 4.1.3 Compute-IT for a different but similar task?

Compute-IT

4.1.5 In pairs, again decide who is going to be the robotic arm and who is going to provide the instructions. Join together with at least three other pairs and work together to build a paper aeroplane, with each pair responsible for creating an algorithm to complete a small part of the process.

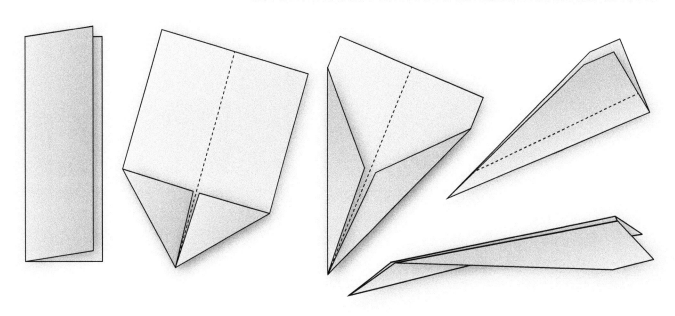

▲ Can you write an algorithm to describe how to make a paper aeroplane?

Think-IT

4.1.6   Think about 4.1.5 Compute-IT.

a)   What challenges did you face when implementing your algorithm as part of a bigger assembly production line?

b)   What can you learn from studying how dancers work together to help you to debug algorithms and fit smaller algorithms into bigger routines?

Think-IT

4.1.7   a)   Sort the tasks below into two groups:

- Tasks best completed by a human
- Tasks best completed by a computer

b)   Explain the thinking behind your choices.

Writing a letter to a friend

Cooking a meal

Making cars

Managing traffic lights

Teaching a primary school class

Painting a picture

Calculating a route

Changing a nappy

Writing a poem

Monitoring a process in a chemical plant

Plan-IT

4.1.8   To complete the challenge you first need to choose a music video that contains a dance routine that you can animate. Once you have done that, record the list of dance moves you are going to recreate, just as you did for 4.1.1 Compute-IT. These will become steps in the algorithm that will form the basis of your animation.

4.2 Sequences, iteration and procedures

Using sequences

The algorithms you created to draw an abstract shape in Unit 3 used a **sequence** of instructions to describe the process. This is the simplest form of algorithm.

When you watch a dance video you should be able to recognise patterns, to see that sequences of dance moves are repeated to form the full routine.

To make a robot in a factory, or a dancer, repeat a sequence over and over again we use **iteration**, placing the sequence inside a loop that continues until we stop it.

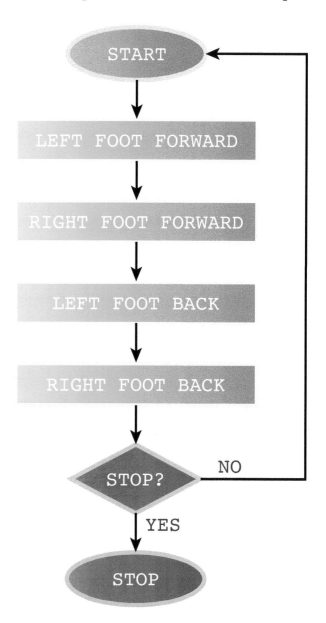

◄ An iterative flowchart showing a simple sequence of dance steps

▲ In Scratch, there is a block called a 'forever' loop that will execute the same set of instructions repeatedly until you end the process. This is what it looks like in Scratch 2.0.

Compute-IT

4.2.1 **a)** Using a graphical programming language and the sequence of dance moves you created for 4.1.8 Plan-IT, program a dance sequence where the sprite returns to the start position at the end of the sequence.

b) Think back to what you have learned already in this unit about timing. Add 'wait' commands to control the speed of the movements and adjust the wait values to produce a realistic dance sequence.

c) Put this sequence inside a 'forever' loop.

d) Search for some suitable music to accompany your dance routine and add this to your program.

Procedures and functions

Procedures and **functions** are a way of abstracting a sequence of instructions, so that you can call on it to execute whenever you need it to without having to repeat the whole sequence each time.

If you ask someone to make a cheese sandwich you are using abstraction because you don't provide him or her with the full list of instructions. You assume they already know that they have to lay out two slices of bread, butter them, slice the cheese and lay it on one piece of the bread, and then place the second slice of bread on top.

In a similar way, if each dance sequence is defined as a procedure, you can call on the sequence of instructions in that procedure each time you want to repeat it. This process is called **procedural abstraction**.

Procedures and functions are therefore sections of code that can be used over and over again. Both can accept input from other parts of the program, but a function can also return information back to other parts of the program. One way to explain this is by looking at an example in Scratch.

Key Terms

Procedure: A procedure is a sequence of program instructions that have been abstracted and can be used over and over again. It can accept input from other parts of the program.

Function: Like a procedure, a function is a sequence of program instructions that have been abstracted and can be used over and over again. Again, like a procedure, it can accept input from other parts of the program, but it can also return information back to other parts of the program.

Procedural abstraction: Hiding the detail of a process in a named procedure or function.

Both these programs produce the same result, but the code in the block under the green flag in the screenshot on the right calls for input from two procedures, one called 'drum' and one called 'direction'. Using procedures reduces the amount of code needed.

You can pass data into a procedure from other parts of the program, and this data can be different every time you use the procedure. For example, the first 'drum' in this program has a 1 next to it. This 1 is passed into the drum type variable in the procedure so that when the program comes to play the drum it looks to see what number has been passed to it and plays drum 1. The second time it comes to play the drum it looks to see what number has been passed to it and plays drum 2, and so on.

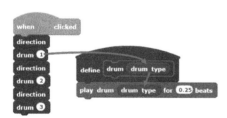

Direction is a simpler procedure, which doesn't have any data passed to it from other parts of the program. It uses the random command three times to change the direction of the sprite and its position on the screen.

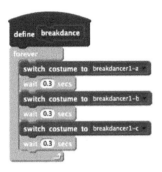

▲ In this example, programmed in Scratch 2.0, the breakdancing sequence of a dance routine is saved as a procedure called 'breakdance' in the first screenshot. It has a 'forever' loop so the sequence will repeat forever.

▲ In the second screenshot you can see how the 'breakdance' procedure and a second procedure called 'dancebreak' are called on by the main program to execute in sequence. The 'forever' loop has been removed so you can control how many times the sequences are executed: 'breakdance' runs five times and then 'dancebreak' runs twice.

Plan-IT

4.2.2 Model the dance routine you are planning to animate by drawing a flow diagram that identifies and refers to one or more procedures for each dance sequence in the routine.

Compute-IT

4.2.3 Using the flow diagram you created for 4.2.2 Plan-IT and the example of a breakdancing program shown above, use sprite costumes to create at least two procedures and combine them together into a dance routine in a graphical programming language.

Plan-IT

4.2.4 Using the list of dance moves you wrote down from your chosen video, you and a partner can create the necessary sprite costumes by taking images of yourself performing each of the dance moves and importing them into your graphical programming language. Or you could find suitable images or sprites to represent the dance moves.

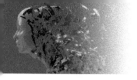

4.3 Selection

Using selection

Before you leave for school each morning, you might look out of the window to see if it is raining so you can decide whether you need to take an umbrella with you. If it is not raining, you will not take an umbrella, but if it is raining, you will take an umbrella. You select your course of action – taking or not taking your umbrella – based on the weather conditions.

Computer programs use **selection** in a similar way, to provide possible courses of action that will be selected as a result of certain conditions being met.

> **Key Term**
>
> **Selection**: The choice of which route to take through a computer program.

An 'if' statement is used to introduce selection into a program. Using a 'forever' block in a graphical programming language means that the program will check forever to see if the conditions have been met and will act accordingly.

When you watch a dance video you can see that sequences of dance moves are repeated to form the full routine, and selection is used to decide which sequences are repeated when and in what order. A program that recreates a realistic dance routine will include a number of different sequences that are repeated according to a selected pattern.

Introducing 'if then else' statements

A type of selection you can use to create your dance routine is called an 'if then else' statement. An 'if then else' statement can be used when you want one procedure to run if one condition is fulfilled, and another procedure to run if it is not. For example, if the chorus is playing in the song run the chorus dance sequence, otherwise (else) run the verse dance sequence.

▲ This screenshot shows how to program an 'if then else' statement in Scratch 2.0. If it is raining, then show umbrella, else hide the umbrella.

Using variables

In this example, programmed in Scratch 2.0, you can see how the 'breakdance' procedure and a second procedure called 'dancebreak' are called on by the main program to execute in sequence.

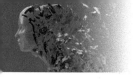
The two dance sequences are repeated a fixed number of times. If you want to reuse these sequences in other dance routines where they are repeated a different number of times, you can replace the fixed repetition with a variable. You can ask the user to input how many times they want to repeat 'breakdance' and how many times they want to repeat 'dancebreak' and their answers will determine how many times the sequences are executed.

ask What's your name? and wait

▲ In Scratch 2.0, the input blocks are called 'ask' blocks.

The next example uses two variables, 'BD' and 'DB', to store the input from the user. They identify the number of times the user wants the procedures 'breakdance' and 'dancebreak' to execute, respectively.

Compute-IT

4.3.1 Create two dance sequences as procedures. Then use a 'forever' block to create a program that plays the first sequence until a certain key is clicked to begin the second sequence. You have now created an algorithm for a simple dance routine and have added both iteration and selection to it.

Challenge

Do you remember the challenge set at the beginning of the unit: to program an animation that recreates a dance routine from a music video using programming techniques such as sequences, iteration, procedures, selection and variables?

Compute-IT

4.3.2 You are now equipped with the computational thinking skills and basic programming constructs to complete the challenge using a graphical programming language and the images you have chosen or taken.

Remember to use what you learnt in Unit 3 about motion/movement instructions so that your sprites can perform their procedures in different parts of the stage, as they would in a real performance to entertain the whole audience.

Create the individual dance sequences as procedures and use these procedures to create the animation. Remember what you have learnt about pattern identification and abstraction; start with a small part of the dance routine and build on it. If you are feeling confident, why not attempt to animate the more complicated parts of the dance routine?

Challenge

Computers simply follow the instructions given to them, so we need to convert the instructions given by humans into something the computer can understand. Your challenge is to write a program to carry out simple arithmetic calculations in a language the machine can understand and to think like the machine in order to do this.

5.1 The origins of modern digital computing

Computer pioneers

Before the development of general-purpose computers, most calculations were undertaken by humans. However, using aids to calculate or compute goes back thousands of years.

The Antikythera is believed to be the earliest mechanical analog 'computer' and is dated around 100BC. It is a complex mechanism designed by the Greeks to calculate the position of the Sun and Moon, the Moon phases, eclipses and the location of various planets in the sky; but until the 1980s we had no idea how it actually worked!

The French mathematician and physicist Blaise Pascal built the first mechanical calculating machine in 1645. This machine used a series of dials and geared wheels to add and subtract.

▲ Antikythera mechanism, dated 100BC

Around 1672, a German called Gottfried Wilhelm von Leibniz developed Pascal's machine further, making the Step Reckoner, which could perform all four arithmetical operations. He did not want men 'to lose hours like slaves in the labour of calculation' when a machine could do it instead.

▲ Pascal's wheel, dated 1645

The first programmable devices were weaving looms. In 1725, a French weaver, Basile Bouchon, used holes in rolls of paper to allow needles in the loom to engage or be held back. The design was later improved by another Frenchman, Joseph-Marie Jacquard, who used punched cards to control each line of the weave. These cards could control over 1000 needles at once and intricate designs could be created and repeated. This development, in 1800, allowed programs to be stored.

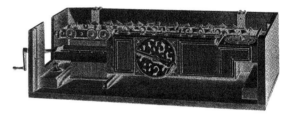

▲ Step Reckoner (Stepped Reckoner), dated 1672

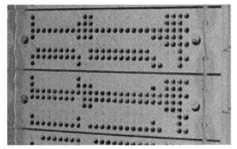

▲ Jacquard punched cards, dated 1800

▲ Babbage's analytical machine, dated 1834

In 1834, Charles Babbage designed the analytical engine, a mechanical device remarkably similar to the modern computer. However, he was too far ahead of his time, and could not finish the work. His design had a central arithmetic unit for calculating (a mill), an area for retaining numbers (a store) and methods for input and output.

Think-IT

5.1.1   Can you see the similarities between Babbage's analytical machine and the model for a computer system you met on page 6 in Unit 1?

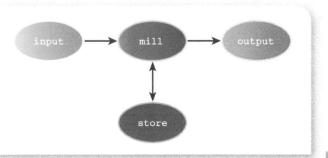

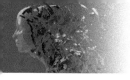

Ada Lovelace

Lord Byron's daughter, Ada, Countess of Lovelace, became fascinated with Babbage's ideas. She wrote an algorithm for Babbage's analytical engine to compute a mathematical problem called Bernoulli numbers, which requires the use of branching to perform a decision, and repetitions to create loops. This is considered the first algorithm specifically designed to work on a computer and Ada is often thought of as the first computer programmer, but her work was not tested as Babbage never completed his analytical engine.

Herman Hollerith and IBM

Dr Herman Hollerith was hired by the US census bureau to create a machine to analyse the data from the 1890 census. He developed Jacquard's ideas and used punched cards to represent the data collected. The position of the hole on the card represented specific information. Where there was a hole in the card a pin was able to pass through and complete an electronic circuit, recording the data on a dial. The census analysis was completed in two years rather than the eight years it had taken to analyse the 1880 census, saving the US treasury millions of dollars. The company that Hollerith formed grew rapidly and when he retired one of his employees took over, renaming the company International Business Machines (IBM) in 1924. IBM currently employs over 400 000 people in a global IT business, manufacturing and selling software and hardware.

Collossus

Advances in electronics in the 1930s led scientists to believe in a true electronic calculating machine and in 1943, spurred on by the need to decipher encrypted messages during the Second World War, Tommy Flowers and Max Newman helped to design and build Colossus, widely regarded as the first fully electronic, programmable binary computer.

Colossus was built specifically for just one task, decrypting ciphers. It was not a general-purpose machine.

▲ Tommy Flowers

ENIAC

The first general-purpose machine was completed in 1946 by Dr John Mauchly and his student, J. Presper Eckert, at the University of Pennsylvania. ENIAC (Electronic Numerical Integrator and Computer) was used for calculating missile trajectories, to predict the weather and in a range of other scientific applications.

▲ ENIAC, dated 1946

The Manchester Baby

The Manchester Small-Scale Experimental Machine, nicknamed The Manchester Baby, is regarded as the world's first stored-program computer. The first program ran in June 1948. It had just 17 instructions and took 52 minutes to reach the correct answer. The Manchester Baby became the Manchester Mark 1, which in turn was the prototype for the Ferranti Mark 1 (Manchester Electronic Computer), which became the world's first commercially available general-purpose electronic computer in February 1951.

▲ The Manchester Baby, dated 1948

▲ Ferranti Mark 1, dated 1951

Compute-IT

5.1.2 Draw a timeline showing the development of the general-purpose computer between 1800 and 2000. Illustrate the timeline with suitable text and images.

Computer generations

Vacuum tubes

▲ Vacuum tubes

The original binary 'first generation' computers, built from 1946 to 1955, used vacuum tubes (valves) for processing. These vacuum tubes were large and used a lot of electricity. ENIAC weighed 30 tons and was almost 25 metres long, 6 metres wide and 3 metres high. It was so power-hungry it was said that every time it was turned on the lights in Philadelphia dimmed.

The transistor

In 1946, William Shockley co-invented the transistor. It did the same job as the vacuum tube, but used a lot less electricity. From 1953 to 1963 these second generation computers got steadily smaller and more efficient. While the first generation computers were programmed using switches and patch leads, second-generation computers used assembly languages. These used simple words, such as 'ADD num', instead of binary for programming. The first **high-level programming languages**, COBOL and FORTRAN, were developed during this period.

▲ A second-generation computer

Key Term

High-level programming language: A programming language which is more abstracted, so easier to read and write and therefore more user-friendly.

The integrated circuit

The development of the integrated circuit brought about the third generation of computers between 1964 and 1970. The integrated circuit is a small 'chip' made from silicon with complete electronic circuits manufactured directly onto them. This generation of computers no longer used punched cards and printers for input and output, but now had keyboards and monitors. These machines could run many different applications at once, and were still smaller and more efficient than their predecessors.

▲ An integrated circuit

The microprocessor

The microprocessor heralded the fourth generation of computers from 1971 to 1991. These were the first personal computers, where the whole computer processor was manufactured onto a single chip. This generation of computers saw the development of graphical user interfaces, the mouse and handheld devices.

▲ A microprocessor

The multi-core processor

The fifth generation of computers, from 1992 to the present, are characterised by their use of much more powerful integrated circuits. These circuits contain two or more independent central processing units called 'cores'. For example, a quad processor has four processing cores, and program instructions are processed in parallel. There has also been a change of use. Computers, which were once used purely for scientific or business purposes, are now in personal use by individuals, largely as a result of the world wide web.

Compute-IT

5.1.3 Add the five generations of computers to the timeline you created in 5.1.2 Compute-IT.

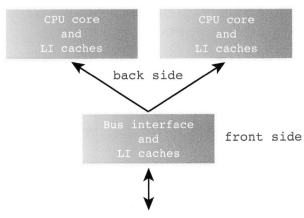

▲ Diagram of a multi-core processor

▲ A multi-core processor

Compute-IT

5.1.4 There are several key people from the history of computing identified in this unit. Here is a list of more names:

John Backus	Grace Hopper	Linus Titus Torvalds
Tim Berners-Lee	Steve Jobs	Alan Turing
George Boole	Brian Wilson Kernighan	John Von Neumann
Kathleen Booth	Peter Naur	Maurice Wilkes
Seymour Cray	Dennis Ritchie	Sophie Wilson
Edsger Dijkstra	Jean Sammet	Jeanette Wing
Stephen Furber	Claude Shannon	Niklaus Wirth
Bill Gates	Stephanie 'Steve' Shirley	Steve Wozniak

a) Choose five people from this list or from elsewhere in this unit, and identify their main contribution to computing.

b) Select one of your chosen five and prepare a presentation about their achievements.

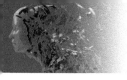

5.2 Programming the machine

Machine instructions

In 1936, Alan Turing published a set of rules for a theoretical machine that were to form the basis for the modern programmable computer.

John Von Neumann used Turing's ideas to formulate a basic set of principles that have been used to define most modern computers ever since. In the Von Neumann architecture, all program instructions and data are stored together (in binary form) in the computer's memory

Originally computers were programmed using switches and patch leads. Since every computer was built individually, every computer had a different set of programming instructions for completing the same task. This is still true today of CPUs: most require different binary codes and different machine instructions to carry out the same task.

▲ Alan Turing

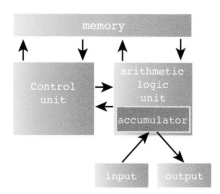

▲ Diagram of Von Neumann Architecture

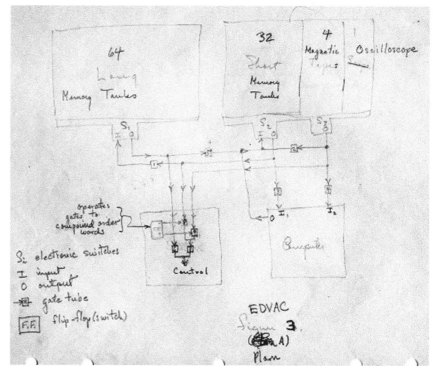

▲ An EDVAC programming panel

A machine instruction has two parts:

- An instruction to do something, which is called the '**operator**'.
- Information on the data or memory location where the instruction should be carried out, which is called the '**operand**'.

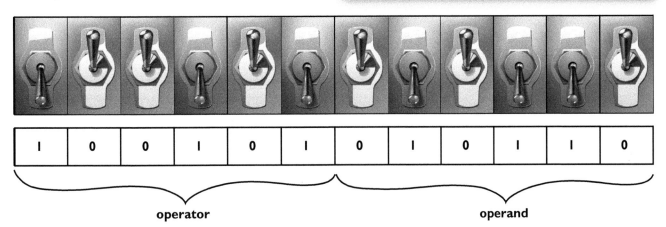

| I | 0 | 0 | I | 0 | I | 0 | I | 0 | I | I | 0 |

operator   operand

Assembly languages

Increasing use of computers led to the development of **assembly languages**. These are easy-to-remember codes, based on the machine's binary instruction set, which can be entered into a computer and translated into the appropriate executable machine instruction by the assembler.

The instruction   **100101010110**

might become   STA NUM1

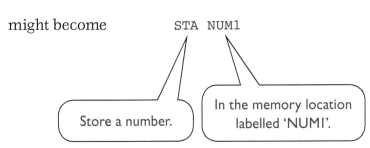

Store a number.

In the memory location labelled 'NUM1'.

One assembly language instruction is the same as one machine instruction. A compiled high-level language program might have several machine instructions to carry out for each high-level instruction.

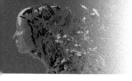

Key Terms

Accumulator: The name given to the place where the computer does all its calculations.

Note: Instructions such as `INP` and `OUT` automatically refer to the accumulator so the operand does not need to be specified.

Variable: A named location in memory used to store data.

If, for example, an assembly language has the following instructions for inputting and outputting values:

`INP`	meaning wait for an input from the user and copy it into the **accumulator**
`OUT`	meaning output whatever value is in the accumulator to the user
`HLT`	meaning halt, because we must always tell the program when to stop
`DAT NUM`	meaning label a memory location with the name 'NUM' to use as a place to store data. 'NUM' is a **variable**, a named location in memory used to store data.

then we can write a very simple program to get an input from the user, store it in memory and then output it:

`INP`	Input a number from the user and copy it to the accumulator.
`STA NUM1`	Store that number in the memory location called 'NUM1'.
`OUT`	Output the number in the accumulator to the user.
`HLT`	Halt.
`NUM1 DAT`	Label this memory location as 'NUM1' to store data.

This set of instructions is put into memory locations. For example:

Memory location	Contents
0	INP
1	STA NUM1
2	OUT
3	HLT
4	NUM1 DAT
5	

> Notice NUM1 DAT is in memory location 4. This means that when we refer to 'NUM1', the computer will look in memory location 4 to get a value.

The user types the codes into files using editors that place them directly into memory locations. The program will do nothing until it is executed or run, at which point it executes each instruction in turn until it is told to stop, using the `HLT` instruction. There is also a special area that keeps track of the next instruction to complete, called the program counter.

A diagram of the CPU after we have written our simple program looks like this:

program counter		memory	
		0	INP
accumulator		1	STA NUM1
		2	OUT
INPUT	OUTPUT	3	HLT
		4	NUM1 DAT
		5	

Think-IT

5.2.1 Copy the table below and dry run the simple program above, writing down what is in each location in the CPU at each stage. The first two lines have been completed for you.

Instruction	Program counter	Accumulator	Input	Output	NUM1
0	1	5	5	–	–
1	2	5	–	–	5

Remember the program counter stores the location of the **next** instruction.

If we add two more commands to the programming language:

ADD FIRST — meaning add whatever you find in the memory location labelled FIRST to whatever is already in the accumulator

SUB FIRST — meaning subtract whatever you find in the memory location labelled FIRST from whatever is already in the accumulator

Then we can input two numbers and add them or subtract one from the other.

Compute-IT

5.2.2 Write a simple program to add together two numbers and dry run it to see if it works. Use 5 and 7 as the input values.

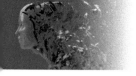

5.3 How the CPU runs a program

How the CPU works

The CPU processes a simple assembly language program using memory locations, input, output, an accumulator and a program counter, but the data needs to be carefully controlled if the machine is to process it correctly. There are therefore two more important features of a CPU that are vital for it to work correctly: the memory address register and the memory data register.

When an instruction refers to an item of data, such as NUM1, the real location of NUM1 in the memory is put into the memory address register.

The accumulator cannot directly access memory locations. It must take data from the memory data register. Putting the location of the data in the memory address register prompts the CPU to move the data it finds in this location (1) into the memory data register (2) so that the accumulator can access it (3).

Our diagram for a CPU now looks like this:

Think-IT

5.3.1 Add two more columns to the dry-run table you created for 5.2.2 Compute-IT, one for the memory address register (MAR) and one for the memory data register (MDR), and complete them.

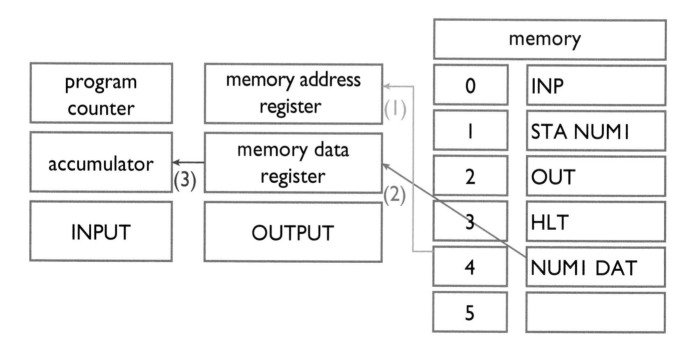

Challenge

Do you remember the challenge at the beginning of the unit, to write a program to carry out simple arithmetic calculations in a language a computer can understand?

We use algebra in mathematics to represent unknown numbers with letters, for example $a + b$ or $a - c$. The letters a, b and c are variables, just like NUM1, and we can write a program in the language the machine understands using some simple commands and variables to make the computer perform as a very simple calculator.

We have already learned how to add two numbers together, but what about calculating the value of $a + b - c$?

We need two more commands for our assembly language to help us to do this:

SUB THIRD	meaning subtract the value in memory location THIRD from the value in the accumulator.
LDA FOURTH	meaning load the value in memory location FOURTH into the accumulator.

Plan-IT

5.3.2 Write an algorithm to show how we can calculate $a + b - c$ by inputting values for a, b and c into our program and having our program output the result.

HINT: Do this calculation on a calculator first and note the key presses. For example, $3 + 5 - 2$ requires us to press:

We enter $3 + 5$ and get the result before subtracting the 2 and outputting the result.

Compute-IT

5.3.3 a) Write the assembly language program to calculate a + b − c and test it with values a = 5, b = 7 and c = 3 and with values a = 6, b = 3 and c = 8.

b) Now work out how to do the same calculation with just one variable, rather than three.

Key Terms

Internet: The internet is a global network of millions of connected computers.

Server: A computer connected to a network (possibly the internet) that manages requests to access its digital services and data.

Artefact: A man-made object, which is of educational, cultural or historical interest. Not all digital resources are man-made, and so are not true artefacts.

Client: A computer connected to a network (possibly the internet) that can request data and process services made available by a server.

Challenge

Your challenge is to research efficiently and effectively three programming languages named after famous people.

6.1 What is the web?

The internet

The **internet** started out as a system called 'ARPANET'. This was the name given to the computer hardware and software that connected the computers at a number of universities and research laboratories in the USA. It was a US Department of Defense project to allow these institutions to share research.

Servers

Servers can be thought of as being like libraries, which are repositories of **artefacts** such as books. Servers store digital data. **Client** computers connect to servers to access the stored data – they are like the people who visit libraries to borrow books or other items. A web page is an example of data stored on a server. A person wishing to access a web page stored on a server will typically do so by connecting to the internet and using a client **web browser** to display the web page data.

Libraries within a geographical area work as a group, so that if a person requests an item that isn't available in their local library then the request is passed to another library within the library group. Similarly, servers and their clients form **networks** of computers that can communicate with each other electronically to provide services and to share data.

At the heart of the internet is the 'backbone', a network of super-powerful computers, known as 'a Tier 1 network'. These computers route all the internet requests that flow between servers and clients. Most belong to governments

Think-IT

6.1.1 List the different types of resources (man-made or otherwise) and services that you can access from both a library and the internet.

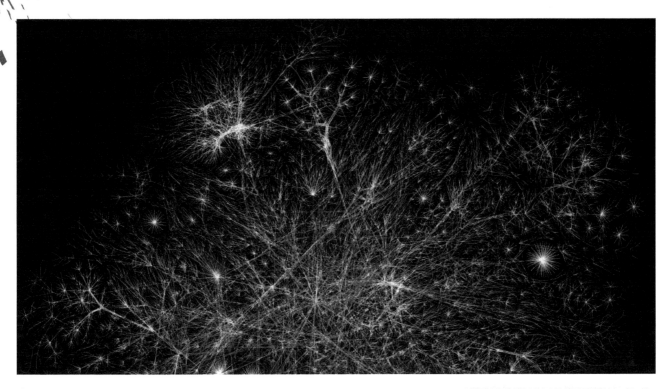

▲ A graphical map of the internet – each line represents a connection between devices.

and universities, who feel it is their duty to contribute to the smooth running of the internet, and do not run the backbone for profit.

The main purpose of the internet is to make sure that two devices that want to share data can find each other, regardless of how far they are from each other and regardless of how busy they are. The internet is a 'network of networks'. Without the internet, a computer can only communicate to other directly connected computers, in the same room or organisation.

The internet is more than the world wide web

Different servers do different things. You connect to an email server to get your emails, to a web server to use the world wide web and to a music streaming server to access services such as Spotify®. A weather sensor installed in the Arctic will connect to the internet to send the data it collects to the university department that is monitoring it. A VOIP (Voice Over Internet Protocol) device, such as Skype™, lets you make a voice or video call over the internet, so you can speak to friends on the other side of the world without the long-distance charges you would incur if you used a telephone line to make the same call.

Key Terms

Web browser: An application that can be used to display information stored digitally as web pages on computers on the world wide web. Google® Chrome and Microsoft® Internet Explorer® are examples of web browsers.

Network: A group of inter-connected computers and the communication infrastructure that allows digital data and services to be shared electronically.

Think-IT

6.1.2 List as many devices as you can that connect to the internet. Which ones involve the world wide web?

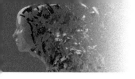
The web

The **world wide web** (**www** or **the web** for short) is a popular service on the internet. It is a chaotic collection of web pages available for everybody to see or hear. Despite the fact that all the web pages are very different and are created by lots of different people or machines working independently, they are all linked together by a system of hyperlinks, enabling you to search for information by moving from one web page to another. This helps you to pool information and share your thoughts and discoveries with the rest of the world.

Hypertext Markup Language

Web pages stored on web servers are written in a special format – often this is **Hypertext Markup Language** (**HTML**) – and it is this which makes it possible to view web pages on the internet. Markup languages consist of instructions that are inserted into documents to tell a computer how to display the information in such a way that web browsers can interpret it. Unlike regular programming languages, markup languages don't perform any calculations; they are just used for formatting and organising digital resources.

▲ HTML documents, known as web pages, are most commonly accessed via a client web browser. Apple Safari®, Mozilla Firefox® and Google® Chrome are popular web browsers

Hypertext uses hyperlinks that allow connections to be made between different web pages or within the same web page, and this goes back to the days when most files on computers were displayed in plain text. Instead of directly placing a picture into a file, you inserted instructions that identified where to find the picture and how to view it. Hyperlinks enable you to navigate between different resources – text, images, videos and other media – just as you might go from library to library accessing books.

It's a small world

We are all part of a number of social groups, each of which are relatively small. Each person's social groups are slightly different, so you are connected to other people you don't know through the people you know in common. The small-world theory says that we are all connected to one another through this network of relationships, and this phenomenon has been given the name 'six degrees of separation'.

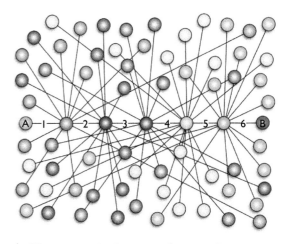

▲ There are six degrees of separation between person A and person B.

Think-IT

6.1.3 What services might be available to you in the future to allow you to model your social networks? What are the possible benefits and drawbacks of such services?

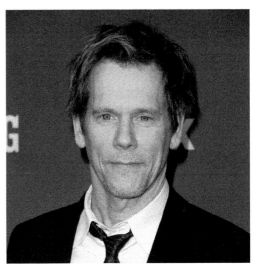

▲ Kevin Bacon, a Hollywood actor

Compute-IT

6.1.4 Kevin Bacon is a Hollywood actor who once famously said that he had probably played in a movie with every other Hollywood actor. He was almost right. Scientists found that most actors can be linked to Kevin Bacon, either directly by having acted in a movie with him, or indirectly if they have been in a movie with someone who has been in a movie with Kevin Bacon.

Type 'Kevin Bacon number' into a search engine and find a web page to help you compute the Bacon number for three of your favourite actors.

Plan-IT

6.1.5 Think about the connections you have to other people, such as through Scouting, Guiding, sports, drama clubs and school, or because they are neighbours, family or friends. Draw a diagram to show the connections and interconnections between you and these people.

▲ Sir Tim Berners Lee, the inventor of the world wide web, was invited to participate in the London 2012 Olympic Games Opening Ceremony.

It's who you know …

There is no central authority on the world wide web that decides which page links to which. There is no one way to find information and there are usually many links between interconnected pages. When browsing the web, you usually aim to find the shortest path you can to the content you want, but you don't know what it is until you click it, and two different people can arrive at the same destination via different paths.

Nobody claims that Kevin Bacon is the best or most popular actor, but we are talking about him because he is connected to so many other people. Social connections give a popular person power. When it comes to a web page, its 'popularity' can be measured by the number of other web pages that hyperlink to it. Many search engines use this idea when they rank the web pages they deliver in response to searches. A web page that has a higher number of links or has links to it on more popular web pages will appear higher up the search list. However, it doesn't necessarily mean it is better; just more 'popular'. So it is important to be accurate with search criteria.

What is a URL?

'URL' stands for 'Uniform Resource Locator', which is the technical name for a web address, and it tells you where on the web you can find the digital resource you are looking for.

If you are transferring data securely over a computer network you will see **https://**. The 's' stands for 'secure' and tells you the website has used encryption to keep communications private.

The extensions **cgi**, **php** and **asp** suggest that a dynamic page is created on the server based on interaction with the client. A website with a shopping basket can't know in advance which items a customer will put in the shopping basket, so the path might refer not to the location of a file, but to the location of a computer program – called a script – which generates and updates all the details on the dynamic page as the customer shops.

Web addresses are unique, just like telephone numbers, and, similarly, they are numerical. The text domain names and file paths were created to make it easier for humans to navigate the web. Behind them lie numbers and other characters that direct the web browser to the numerical address of the website. For example, **www.hodder.co.uk** has the numerical address 89.197.122.84.

Key Term

Protocol: A standard set of rules and instructions to be followed by a computer.

This shows the type of server the data is held on. In this instance it is the world wide web.

This is the domain name; the web address of the server that hosts this web page.

This is the file path, which locates the web page on the server's drive. In this example, /computeit is the folder on the server where all the Compute-IT resources are kept for publishing and /bookone is the filename of the web page you want the server to send.

Filenames often have html or htm at the end. This shows you that you are looking at a static page which was created by a web designer.

Together these form the 'prefix': the information before the domain name.

http://www.hoddereducation.co.uk/computeit/bookone.html

This is the name of the protocol the browser should use. It tells the browser how the data is formatted and how it is transmitted. http:// shows the data is hypertext and is being transmitted over a network. Other protocols include ftp and file.

This is the domain suffix. It tells you which country the server hosting the page is in and/or the type of company or organisation which owns it. For example, '.com' signifies a company, '.co.uk' a UK company and '.gov.uk' a UK Government service. New domain suffixes are sometimes introduced. For example, '.tv' is now used for online television. It is possible for one domain name to have two different suffixes, which means that abcompany.co.uk and abcompany.org.uk could belong to two completely different organisations.

Compute-IT

6.1.6 Read the following descriptions of the URLs of several imaginary web pages and reconstruct their likely web addresses. Then state whether the pages are dynamic or static. For example, **about.html** was downloaded from **www.bigserver.co.uk** via the HTML protocol. It was stored on that server in a folder called 'projects', which was, in turn, located in a folder called 'public'. This becomes: **http://www.bigserver.co.uk/public/projects/about.html**. It is a static page.

a) help.html was received via an HTML protocol from the Australian web server bigkoala. It was stored in a folder called 'users'.

b) A web-based php game called Werewolves runs off a commercial web server called happytimes. The page is generated on the fly for each player.

c) Taxinfo is a PDF file that is available for download from the UK Government's web server, from a folder called 'forms', which is located in another folder called '2013'.

Compute-IT

6.1.7 There are companies on the web that offer a service to shorten URLs, so that you don't have to remember long strings of letters and numbers. They work by adding the URL to a list and then returning a shortened 'alias' URL such as **http://tinyurl.com/pr433fn**. If the service has previously received a request to shorten a URL, then it will return the existing shortened alias URL rather than creating a new, duplicate, alias. Go to **http://tinyurl.com** and follow the instructions to enter a long URL of your choice and see what comes out.

6.2 How do we know what to trust on the web?

EFFECTIVENESS = RELEVANCE + QUALITY

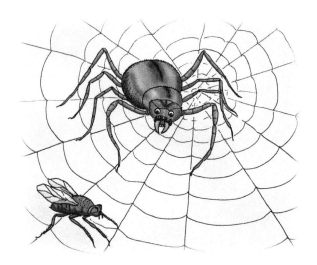

Bogus websites: take care out there

The physical world is full of parasites and predators and the world wild web is no different.

Cybersquatting and typosquatting

Cybersquatters register domain names that are very similar to the names of large companies, brands or celebrities, or they wait until somebody running a popular website forgets to renew their web registration and the cybersquatters buy up the domain name. They then try to profit from their actions, often by trying to sell the domain names to the company, brand or person affected for a large sum of money.

Typosquatting is more sinister. Typosquatters register slightly misspelt versions of popular domain names, hoping to divert people from the genuine website to their fake website. Once you are on the fake website they have lots of ways to make money out of your mistake. For example, they might receive advertising revenue from the adverts that you see, or they might trick you into sharing valuable personal information or picking up a virus.

Compare

```
● ● ●
◉ ◉ ◉  www.britain.com
```

with

```
● ● ●
◉ ◉ ◉  www.britian.com
```

Thin content

Thin content pages don't have useful content of their own. They are just full of links that push visitors to other web pages and they get paid for every click-through they generate. Often thin content pages live on abandoned websites, also known as parked sites, which are filled with random, low-quality sales links from dishonest sellers or for unreliable products.

Content farms

Content farms have a high advert-to-content ratio. This means that they contain a lot more adverts than useful text. Often content farms have been built in a hurry with little effort, even repeating text to make the website appear larger and more useful than it actually is.

Spam web pages

Spam web pages are used to manipulate search engine results. They want you to click through to as many of the pages to which they provide links as possible, because they get paid for people viewing banners and clicking through to other websites. The content on these spam web pages is rarely related. For instance, a spam web page disguised as a web page that sells tablet computers might contain links to dubious web pages.

Think-IT

6.2.1 What makes it possible to create bogus websites?

6.2.2 How do you stay safe on the web and avoid bogus web pages?

Compute-IT

6.2.3 Google provides guidance on how to create effective, high-quality websites. Search for 'Google quality guidelines' and you'll find a list of practices it encourages you to avoid. Follow the links in the list and note down, for each practice, whether you have ever visited websites that do not follow their advice. Can you remember how you ended up at those websites?

Evaluating content on the web

Once you have discounted the bogus (unreliable and untrustworthy) websites, there is still a great deal of fantastic stuff on the web. It is a particularly useful place to gather information about all sorts of subjects, from the latest research on medical advances to facts and figures about pop stars and the achievements of sports men and women. It is important to recognise, however, that there is very little censorship of web content. Alongside all the accurate information there is a lot of unreliable and even incorrect and misleading information available for you to look at.

Fact, opinion and bias

Some websites are written by non-specialists who present their thoughts and ideas on a subject as facts. Other websites are written by very knowledgeable people, but are biased because they present just one side of the story.

Wikipedia was founded in response to the huge quantity of poor-quality and biased information on the web. A 'wiki' is a website developed collaboratively by a community of users and 'pedia' comes from 'encyclopedia', which is a book containing accurate information on a lot of different subjects. Wikipedia prides itself on its lack of bias.

Compute-IT

6.2.4 *Bloomberg Businessweek* is a magazine and website published by Bloomberg, a company that is a leader in global business and financial information. It analysed the money hip-hop artists claim 'in their lyrics' to have and their actual wealth. Visit **http://tinyurl.com/k2yl3p8** to see what they discovered. Look at the information for Lil Wayne and 50 cent. Are you surprised?

▲ Wikipedia does not contain any adverts and is run by a not-for-profit foundation.

Wikipedia claims to achieve a lack of bias by having several people, often with opposing views, jointly editing each article. The idea is that if something appears biased, those who disagree with it will remove it or add their side of the story. However, it was recently revealed that some wiki editors don't play by the rules and delete content they don't agree with without producing anything to disprove the things they don't like.

How do you know whether the information on a web page is trustworthy?

It is vitally important to evaluate every website you visit to assess the trustworthiness of the information it contains. Look out for:

- Accuracy: Is the article well researched? Are there facts and figures to back up opinions?
- Currency: When was the article written? Has it been updated recently?
- Author: Is the author named? Is the author qualified to comment on the subject they are writing about? Have they written on the subject before? Can you find other articles they have written on other web pages?
- Hosting website: Is the organisation hosting the website well known and generally considered to be trustworthy?
- Balanced presentation: Are both sides of an argument (the 'pros and cons') covered in equal measure? Does the author acknowledge that there is another point of view on the subject they are writing about and give that point of view appropriate respect?
- Professional tone: Is the article well written? It doesn't have to be hard to understand to have authority, but it will avoid street language, 'textspeak' and 'hip' phrases. It should also avoid inappropriately emotional language.

Above all, get your information from more than one unrelated source. You'll then be able to see what they all agree on, and identify this information as the most accurate. This is the foundation of good critical thinking.

Think-IT

6.2.5 How accurate do you think Wikipedia is as a source of information?

Compute-IT

6.2.6 Go to http://digg.com or www.reddit.com. These are aggregator sites, which collect together interesting web pages from around the world that have been submitted by members. Choose five featured web pages and evaluate their quality.

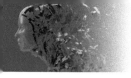

How long does content live on the web?

Usually, when you type a URL into your web browser, you will be taken straight to the website you want. Yet things can sometimes go wrong. Data can be lost or corrupted. Malware, a computer crash, a programming mistake or even a power outage can cause problems. Engineers can even accidentally cut a cable that connects an entire country to the internet. A well-administered website will have a backup of important data, which can be used if something goes wrong.

The cost of storage is so low these days that, in most cases, old web pages, old posts and old news articles are still available on the internet. It is important to realise that, when you search for information, you might find something very old and out of date.

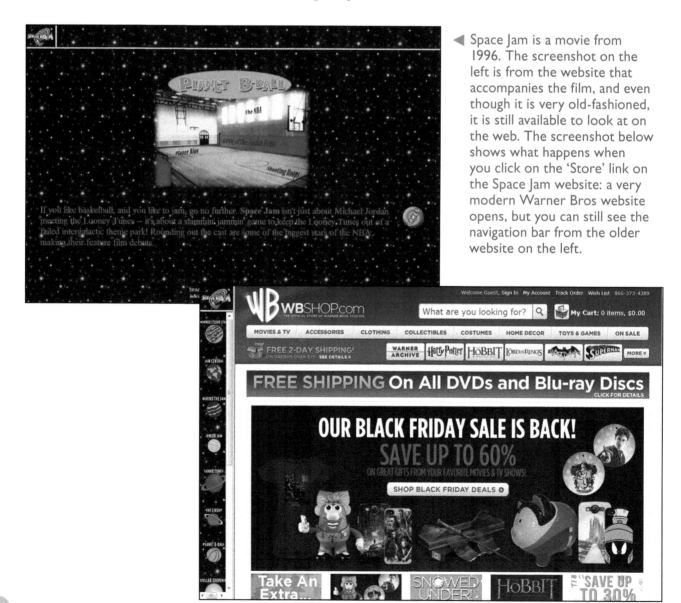

◀ Space Jam is a movie from 1996. The screenshot on the left is from the website that accompanies the film, and even though it is very old-fashioned, it is still available to look at on the web. The screenshot below shows what happens when you click on the 'Store' link on the Space Jam website: a very modern Warner Bros website opens, but you can still see the navigation bar from the older website on the left.

Posts on social media websites when you are young –
including angry and mean messages and photographs
you take of yourself doing something you shouldn't
when you're hanging out with friends – can
and do come back to haunt you many
years later.

Cloud computing is where data is stored
on an internet service called the 'cloud' and
not on your computer. This might increase
the risk of images you think you have deleted
being available for others to see in the future,
especially if you don't select the right privacy
settings for your cloud account.

Are there photos of you online ▶
that you might not want friends
or future employers to see?

Compute-IT

6.2.7 The Internet Way Back Machine
website has been storing snapshots of
websites since 1996. Find out how your
favourite websites have changed over
the years. What has changed and why?

Compute-IT

6.2.8 Geocities was the first giant online
community when it launched in 1994.
When it was closed down in 2009, a
project archived it so you can see it
as it was. Search for 'geocities archive
project' and have a look around. What
has changed and why?

Think-IT

6.2.9 In 2010, *The Telegraph* reported the following:

> *Mr Schmidt [Eric Schmidt of Google] said he believed that every young person will one day
> be allowed to change their name to distance themselves from embarrassing photographs
> and material stored on their friends' social media sites.*

> www.telegraph.co.uk/technology/google/7951269/Young-will-have-to-change-names-to-escape-cyber-
> past-warns-Googles-Eric-Schmidt.html

Some companies now search for an interviewee online and check their Facebook profiles
before hiring them. Is there anything about you on the web that might cost you a job in the
future?

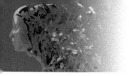

6.3 How do we search the web?

Google page rank

Google® revolutionised searching the web. Before Google, a **search engine** used special web-surfing programs called 'spiders' that crawled around the web loading pages, creating a description of them and then storing this description in a large database known as an 'index'. When you used the search engine it searched the index for characters that matched the characters in your search term and delivered them all to you.

The Google search engine was launched in 1998. It was different because it appeared to deliver more relevant results. It still used spiders to create an index, but it then used page ranking to ensure that the results delivered to you were useful and, more than likely, the ones you wanted.

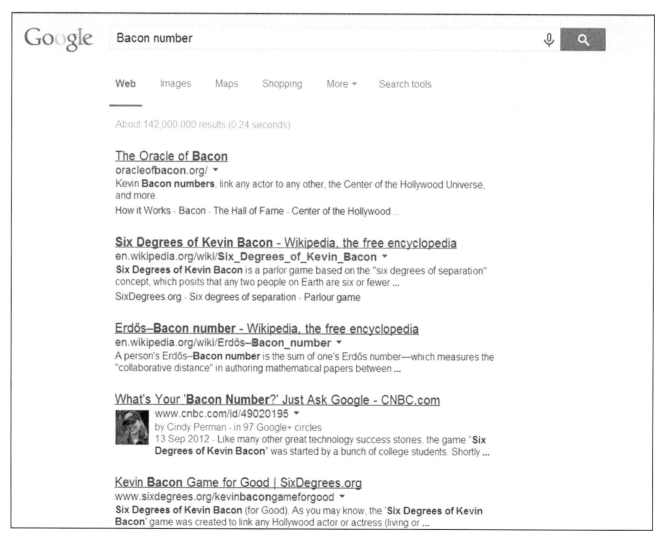

▲ These are the search results returned when 'Bacon number' is typed into Google's search engine.

Home-Links | Netscape/Mozilla Downloads
NEWS: Independent Council Report and Clinton Responses

Aliweb™ [   ] [Search] [Reset]

ADVANCED OPTIONS: Case Sensitive: ☐
Display Fields Other Than Title? ☑ Description ☐ Keyword ☐ URL ☐ Other
Select Search Fields ☑ Title ☑ Description ☑ Keyword ☑ URL
Limit Results To: [20 matches ▼] Restrict to Domain: [none ▼]
Search Type: [Whole Words ▼] Record Type: [Any ▼]

Aliweb Search Results for 'bacon number'

[4] **Department of Mathematics**
    Research, Teaching and Consultancy in the Department of Mathematics at Imperial College, London UK
[4] **Bacon Mansion Bed & Breakfast**
    Bacon Mansion is a local bed and breakfast in the Capitol Hill neighborhood of Seattle with pictures of rooms, maps, food, etc. online.
[2] **Picons Memory Game - Setup**
    The Memory card game implemented in JavaScript, using random picons for pictures. Fully configurable for number of players, number of cards, and pictures used.
[2] **Which program executes faster, assuming that speed is directly proportional to the number of memory accesses needed?**
    Which program executes faster, assuming that speed is directly proportional to the number of memory accesses needed?
[2] **Australian Computer Society (ACS) member viewpoints, and some other documents relating to regulation of the Internet.**
    Includes Andrew Freeman, Director, Community Affairs Board (CAB), ACS's viewpoint on regulation of the Internet. Includes pointers to a number of other ACS members who have expressed views on the regulation of the Internet issue. Also includes pointers to papers on this issue by members of a number of other organisations.
[2] **Versioning Software Systems through Concept Descriptions**

▲ Aliweb is considered by many to be the web's first search engine. It was established in 1993. Look how much more relevant Google's results appear to be.

Page ranking is achieved by an algorithm. It uses hyperlinks between web pages to work out which web pages are the most popular and then it returns these at the top of the list of results it delivers to you. For example, consider web page A and web page B, each about vampires. If ten other web pages link to web page A and five other web pages link to web page B, a search for 'vampires' will return web page A at the top of the list of results.

Smart search terms

In a web context, **Boolean operators** are connective words that manage the results returned from a search. There are three Boolean operators that can be used in a search engine:

Key Term

Boolean operators: For example, the connective words AND, OR and NOT. In the context of searching the web, they manage the results returned.

One way to think about how Boolean operators help you to search efficiently is to imagine your search terms as a Venn diagram.

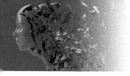

For example, if you wanted to buy a gold necklace using the internet and you entered 'gold AND necklace' into your search engine, your Venn diagram would look like this:

If you knew you wanted to buy a piece of gold jewellery but didn't know whether you wanted a necklace or a bracelet, you would enter 'gold AND necklace OR bracelet' into your search engine and your Venn diagram would look like this:

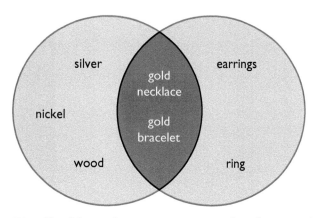

Finally, if you knew you wanted to buy a piece of gold jewellery but the person you are buying it for has said they definitely don't want any more necklaces, you would enter 'gold AND jewellery NOT necklace' into your search engine and your Venn diagram would look like this:

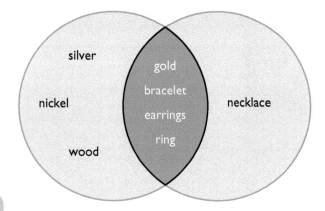

Acknowledging your sources

When you carry out a piece of research you collect information from lots of different sources and you pull it all together to form a coherent essay or presentation. 'Plagiarism' is the name given to the process of using someone else's words, thoughts or ideas and presenting them as your own. It is easy to fall victim to plagiarism when you are using the web, because it is so simple to cut and paste text and images, but it is very easy for teachers and examiners to spot, and you will have a lot of marks deducted and might even fail a piece of work if you do plagiarise other people's work.

Think-IT

6.3.1   What can you do to ensure you avoid plagiarism?

Challenge

Do you remember the challenge at the beginning of this unit? Your task is to efficiently and effectively research three programming languages named after famous people.

Compute-IT

6.3.2   Use Boolean search terms to search the web and find as much relevant and high-quality information as you can about three programming languages named after famous people. You have thirty minutes to complete your task.

Challenge

Your challenge is to design and code a web page and upload it to a server.

Key Term

HyperText Markup Language (HTML): HTML is the main markup language for creating web pages and displaying other information in a web browser. Hyper is from the Greek for 'over' and means that hypertext is more than just text. It is used to reference other text or documents.

7.1 Usable and accessible web pages

HyperText Markup Language (HTML)

Web pages are text documents that can be opened in any text editor. They have **HTML** tags that tell the browser what to do when displaying the page. These tags might include links to images, formatting commands, which tell the browser to display the text in bold or in italics, or links to other web pages. HTML tags wrap around text rather like speech marks, with a / used in the closing tag.

This is the HTML code for the web page above. ▶

Web page usability and accessibility

It is important to think about **usability** and **accessibility** when designing a web page. Usability refers to the process of making a web page quick and easy to navigate. When considering usability, web page designers think about things like how many clicks the user has to make to get to the content they want and where the best place on the screen is for each feature.

Accessibility is all about making sure all users, including those with disabilities, can use the web page. The web page designer will consider, for example, how a person who has limited sight will find their way around the web page features.

Key Terms

Usability: The process of making a web page quick and easy to use.

Accessibility: Accessibility is all about making sure that all users, including those with disabilities, can use the web page.

Think-IT

7.1.1   Look at web pages from a range of different websites. List their similarities and differences and then think about the following:

- Why are menu bars usually at the top of a web page, and not at the bottom or on the right-hand side?
- Why are navigation features usually on the left-hand side of a web page?
- Might these design choices be different for web pages written in Chinese, Arabic or Hebrew?

Plan-IT

7.1.2   Building on the experience you gained completing 7.1.1 Think-IT, sketch the most common web page structure.

Think-IT

7.1.3   Compare the CBBC Newsround website (**www.bbc.co.uk/newsround/news/**) with the BBC News website (**www.bbc.co.uk/news/**). What is it about the CBBC Newsround website that makes it more appealing than the BBC News website to younger children?

Remixing a website for a given audience

X-Ray Goggles is software that enables you to remix web pages easily by clicking on parts of the page you want to change and editing the HTML directly. You can even change the images on a web page to any other picture you have found or uploaded to the web. When you are looking for images, be aware that images and text are stored in different files and the HTML references the image file to display it. It is also important to acknowledge the original source when you use content from other web pages.

Compute-IT

7.1.4   Use X-Ray Goggles or similar software to remix a web page of your choice. Make it as exciting as you can!

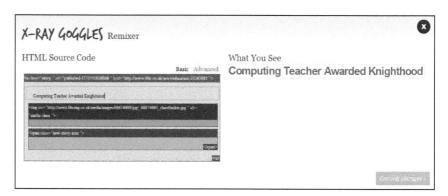

▲ X-Ray Goggles

Plan-IT

7.1.5   Visit the home page of your local news website. How could you make it more appealing to someone of your age? Think back to what you learned about usability and accessibility in 7.1.3 Think-IT as well as:

- the font used (for size and style of text and headers)
- the colour scheme used for the buttons, the background and the font
- the text (how much there is and how interesting, relevant and well placed it is)
- the images used (how many there are and how interesting and well placed they are)
- navigability (how easy it is to navigate). For example, are the buttons in the right places? What if you are blind or visually impaired?
- anything else?

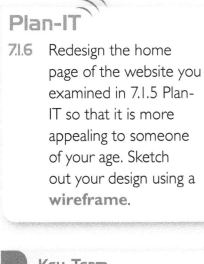

Plan-IT

7.1.6   Redesign the home page of the website you examined in 7.1.5 Plan-IT so that it is more appealing to someone of your age. Sketch out your design using a **wireframe**.

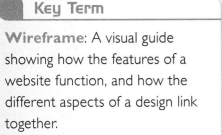

Key Term

Wireframe: A visual guide showing how the features of a website function, and how the different aspects of a design link together.

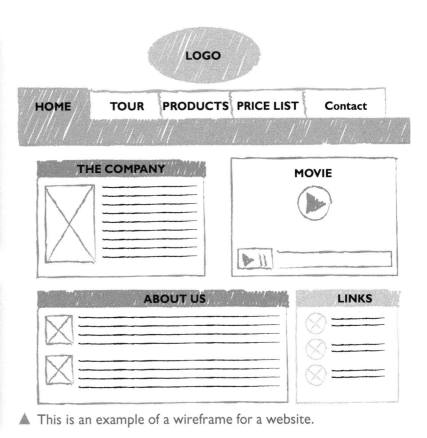

▲ This is an example of a wireframe for a website.

Here are some simple HTML commands, or 'tags', that can be used to enhance a web page.

Headings

Make a heading with:

```
<h1>heading 1</h1>
<h2>heading 2</h2>
<h3>heading 3</h3>
```

It goes all the way down to `<h6>`.

Paragraphs

Make a paragraph with: `<p>put paragraph of text in here</p>`

Add colour to a paragraph with: `<p style="color:orange">`

Colour

You can choose any colour using a colour picker and some hexadecimal numbers, but the standard basic colours are: aqua, **black**, **blue**, fuchsia, gray, green, lime, **maroon**, **navy**, olive, orange, purple, red, silver, teal, white, and yellow.

You can change the background colour too with: `<p style="background-color:olive">`

You can also choose the font by using: `<p style="font-family:sans-serif">`

Fonts

You can choose: serif, **sans-serif**, `monospace`, *cursive* and
fantasy.

Linking tags

Add several instructions together in one tag by linking
them with semi-colons:

```
<p style="color: orange;background-color:olive;font-family:sans-serif">
```

For example:

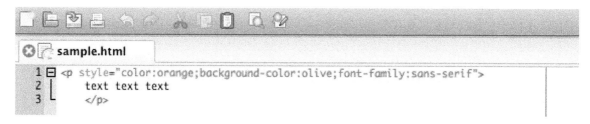

```
sample.html
1 <p style="color:orange;background-color:olive;font-family:sans-serif">
2     text text text
3     </p>
```

Strong and emphasis

Make an important point with:

```
<strong>very important information</strong>
```

Add a little emphasis with:

```
<em>emphasised text</em>
```

Inserting images

An image tag is a special command that links to an image
file:

```
<img src=" http://www.google.com/logos/2006/worldcup06_uk.gif"
alt="WorldCup"
width="276" height="120"
style="float:right;">
```

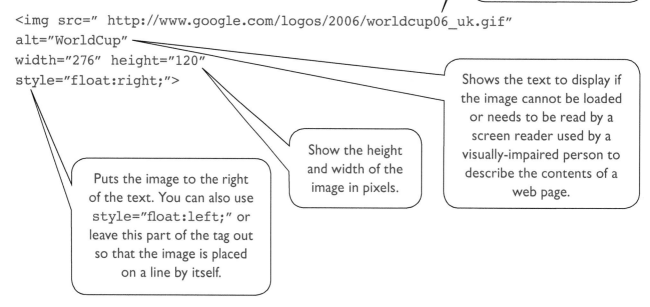

Shows the URL where the image can be found. The .gif shows the image's file type.

Shows the text to display if the image cannot be loaded or needs to be read by a screen reader used by a visually-impaired person to describe the contents of a web page.

Show the height and width of the image in pixels.

Puts the image to the right of the text. You can also use style="float:left;" or leave this part of the tag out so that the image is placed on a line by itself.

`<strong>`And don't forget to close your HTML tags!`</strong>`

Compute-IT

7.1.7   Use a code editor to edit the local news website you thought about in 7.1.6 Plan-IT.

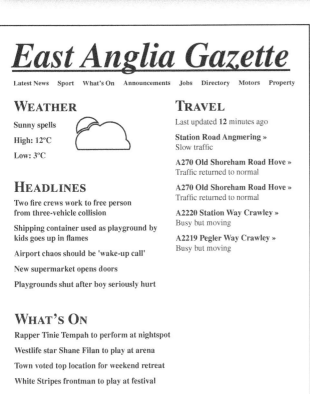

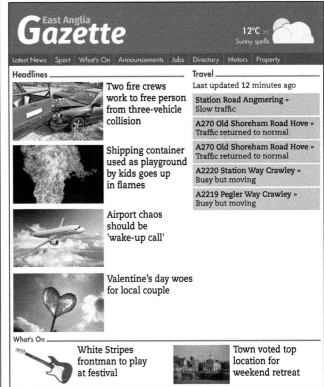

▲ Before: A slow news day in East Anglia

After: The web page looks much more vibrant now, with stronger colours and large images.

Plan-IT

7.1.8   Take the presentation you prepared in Unit 5 about a famous person from the history of computing, and design a web page containing the information you gathered using all the knowledge you now have about usability, accessibility and HTML. Your web page should contain at least one image.

7.2 Making your web page

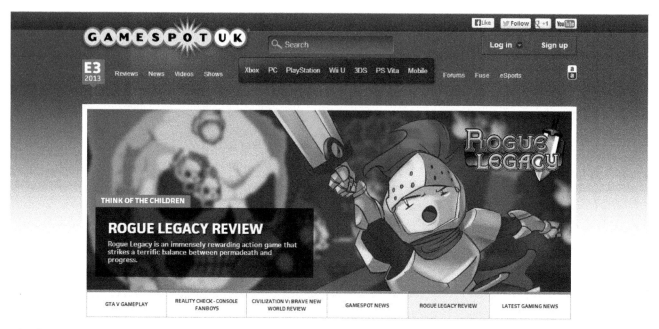

▲ Gamespot won the prestigious Webby Award (**www.webbyawards.com**) for its design and content in 2013.

HTML

Making a beautiful web page starts with beautiful code. Here is an example:

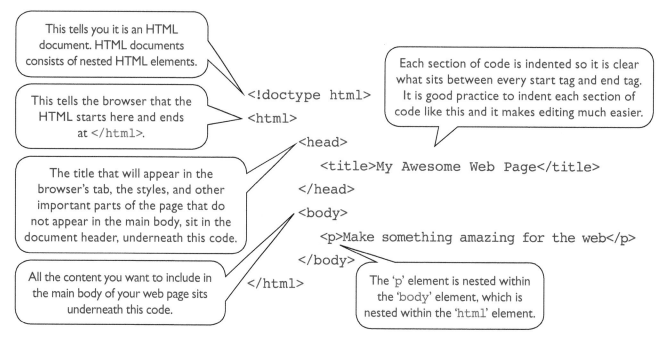

> This tells you it is an HTML document. HTML documents consists of nested HTML elements.

> This tells the browser that the HTML starts here and ends at </html>.

> Each section of code is indented so it is clear what sits between every start tag and end tag. It is good practice to indent each section of code like this and it makes editing much easier.

> The title that will appear in the browser's tab, the styles, and other important parts of the page that do not appear in the main body, sit in the document header, underneath this code.

> All the content you want to include in the main body of your web page sits underneath this code.

> The 'p' element is nested within the 'body' element, which is nested within the 'html' element.

```
<!doctype html>
<html>
    <head>
        <title>My Awesome Web Page</title>
    </head>
    <body>
        <p>Make something amazing for the web</p>
    </body>
</html>
```

HTML was designed to be read by computers and by people, and you can see straight away that the title of the web page coded above is 'My Awesome Web Page' and the content is 'Make something amazing for the web'.

You can give each element on your web page a border.
In this example, the paragraph is given a border:

This is where you note the colour of the border using one of the HTML colours.

This is where you note the thickness of the border in pixels.

```
<p style="border:5px dotted red">
```

This is where you note the style of the border. You can choose from:

| dotted | dashed | solid | double | groove | ridge | inset | outset |

▲ With Mozilla Thimble you can see how your code looks immediately.

Compute-IT

7.2.1 Code the web page you created for 7.1.8 Plan-IT.

Think-IT

7.2.2 Use the skills of **abstraction** and **generalisation** to improve the coding of your web page. Look for common patterns in your code, and think of ways of using these to present a simplified version of the code.

Key Terms

Abstraction: Working with ideas or solving a problem by identifying common patterns in real situations, concentrating on general ideas and not on the detail of the problem itself.

Generalisation: Taking concepts used in the solution of a particular problem and using them to solve other problems that have similar features.

Cascading Style Sheet (CSS)

HTML provides the content for a page, but **Cascading Style Sheets** (**CSS**) provide the format. This means that content can be treated separately from layout. Wherever you have seen `style=` you are using CSS to format your work, but you don't have to code the style for each individual element on your web page because, with CSS, you can also establish a consistent style for a whole web page or website by adding the correct information to the document header. CSS also enables websites to load more quickly, because the files are smaller. There is less code when all the styles are set once at the start, rather than every time an element occurs.

Key Term

Cascading Style Sheets (CSS): Cascading style sheets are used to format the layout of web pages. Styles can be applied to whole websites and web pages, or to individual elements, making things simpler. Any styles applied directly to individual elements will override styles applied to the whole document.

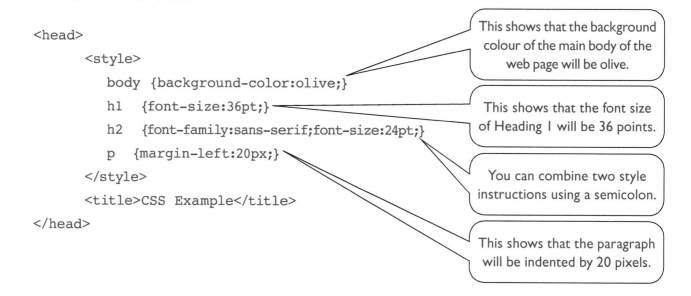

```
<head>
    <style>
        body  {background-color:olive;}
        h1    {font-size:36pt;}
        h2    {font-family:sans-serif;font-size:24pt;}
        p     {margin-left:20px;}
    </style>
    <title>CSS Example</title>
</head>
```

This shows that the background colour of the main body of the web page will be olive.

This shows that the font size of Heading 1 will be 36 points.

You can combine two style instructions using a semicolon.

This shows that the paragraph will be indented by 20 pixels.

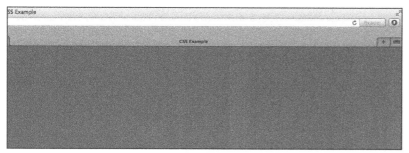

▲ The CSS above generates an olive green page.

Compute-IT

7.2.3 Use CSS to improve the look of the web page you coded for 7.2.1 Compute-IT by setting default styles for the whole web page. Remember to remove the individual style settings you have already coded before coding the default styles in the header.

Automatic format checkers

As with any language, HTML has its own rules of **grammar**, **syntax** and vocabulary that people coding web pages should always follow. Also, it is very easy to make spelling or grammatical errors. It is therefore important to check that you haven't made mistakes. This process is called **verification**.

There are automated tools, called markup validators, that we can use to verify HTML documents. During verification, the tool compares the HTML document produced with the defined syntax of HTML and reports any discrepancies.

One example of a tool that will check the validity of HTML documents is the W3C's Markup Validation Service (**http://validator.w3.org**). The first screenshot shows a web page that has passed validation and the second shows a web page that has failed.

This document was successfully checked as XHTML 1.0 Strict!		
Result:	Passed	
Address:	http://www.w3.org/	
Encoding:	utf-8	(detect automatically)
Doctype:	XHTML 1.0 Strict	(detect automatically)
Root Element:	html	
Root Namespace:	http://www.w3.org/1999/xhtml	

Errors found while checking this document as XHTML + RDFa!		
Result:	35 Errors, 2 warning(s)	
Address:	http://www.bbc.co.uk/	
Encoding:	utf-8	(detect automatically)
Doctype:	XHTML + RDFa	(detect automatically)
Root Element:	html	
Root Namespace:	http://www.w3.org/1999/xhtml	

It is important to remember that a '**valid**' web page isn't automatically a 'good' web page, although an 'invalid' web page is more than likely to be a poor web page. By using a validator and removing errors, you can help to ensure that your HTML documents are displayed correctly in all the main web browsers (including Mozilla Firefox, Google Chrome, Microsoft Internet Explorer and Apple Safari), but you will need to put into practice many other skills to ensure your web page contains high-quality content and is usable and accessible.

Key Terms

Grammar: A set of rules that define the relationships between words in a language.

Syntax: The grammatical arrangement of words in a language, showing how they connect and relate to each other.

Verification: The process of checking that the grammar, syntax and vocabulary of code are correct.

Valid: Something is valid when it is sound, defensible and well grounded. 'Validation' is the name given to the process of checking that something is valid.

Compute-IT

7.2.4 Verify your web page using a markup validator (such the W3C's Markup Validation Service: **http://validator.w3.org**), and correct any errors.

7.3 Bringing content together

Compute-IT

7.3.1 A web browser is a program that interprets HTML code and displays it on your computing device. Some HTML code is shown below. Your task is to interpret the code and draw an artist's impression of what the web page will look like.

```
<!doctype html>
<html>
    <head>
        <style>
            body {background-color:gray; font-size:12pt}
            h1 {font-size:36pt}
            p {margin-left:20px;}
            strong {color:orange; font-size:20pt ;font-family:
            sans-serif}
            em {background-color:green}
        </style>
        <title>Fun Page</title>
    </head>
    <body>
        <h1>The Big Heading</h1>
        <p>This is some <em>very</em> important <strong>text
        </Strong></p>
    </body>
</html>
```

Lists and tables

Being able to make lists and tables are two of the most useful HTML tools. Lists and tables are easier to read than long blocks of text and enable people to get quickly to the key information they are looking for. It is also useful to be able to embed content, like videos, from other websites.

Lists

First, here's how to code an unordered list:

> The key command here is `<ul>`, which shows that the list is unordered and will appear as a bulleted list.

```
<ul>
      <li>Order of items in list does not matter</li>
      <li>It does not matter what the order of the items in the list is</li>
</ul>
```

An ordered list works like this:

> The command `<ol>` shows that the list is ordered and will appear as a numbered list.

```
<ol>
      <li>Most important item</li>
      <li>Second most important item</li>
</ol>
```

- 1802 – **German astronomer** Heinrich Wilhelm Matthias Olbers **discovered 2 Pallas, the second asteroid known to man.**
- 1910 – **Near Martigues, France,** French aviator Henri Fabre's *Fabre Hydravion* **became the first seaplane to take off from water under its own power.**
- 1920 – **An outbreak of 37 tornadoes across the** Midwestern and Southern United States **left more than 380 people dead.**
- 1930 – **Turkey changed the name of its largest city Constantinople to** Istanbul.
- 1979 – **A partial core meltdown of the** Three Mile Island Nuclear Generating Station *(pictured)* near Harrisburg, Pennsylvania, **resulted in the release of an estimated 43,000 curies (1.59 PBq) of radioactive** krypton **to the environment.**

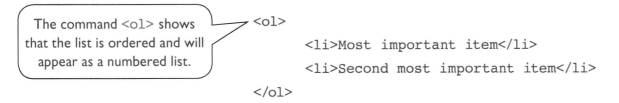

Frequently Asked Questions

1. What is the National Student Survey (NSS)?
2. How are the survey results used?
3. Who is responsible for the survey?
4. When and how does the survey take place?
5. Who will be asked to take part in the survey?
6. What is being asked in the survey?
7. Who has access to eligible students' contact details?
8. Are my responses anonymous?
9. How do I take part in the survey?
10. Can I select my preferred method of re-contact for completing the survey?

- Review hundreds of facts and cement them in your memory
- Understand the wider background with extension information on each fact
- Pinpoint just how much you know - the app tracks your progress!

1. Where can I buy one?
2. How much does it cost?
3. What do I get when I buy one?
4. Why is the price in US Dollars? You are a UK company!
5. Is there a buy-one-give-one program?
6. Is the device available internationally?

▲ Unordered and ordered lists are very useful to display information instructions, or questions.

Tables

Here's how to code a simple table:

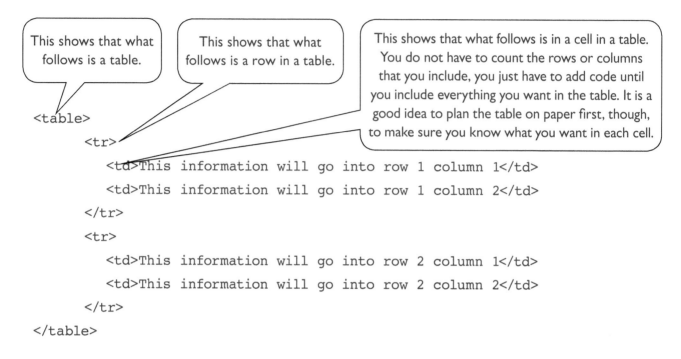

This shows that what follows is a table.

This shows that what follows is a row in a table.

This shows that what follows is in a cell in a table. You do not have to count the rows or columns that you include, you just have to add code until you include everything you want in the table. It is a good idea to plan the table on paper first, though, to make sure you know what you want in each cell.

```
<table>
    <tr>
        <td>This information will go into row 1 column 1</td>
        <td>This information will go into row 1 column 2</td>
    </tr>
    <tr>
        <td>This information will go into row 2 column 1</td>
        <td>This information will go into row 2 column 2</td>
    </tr>
</table>
```

The coded table will look like this: This information will go into row 1 column 1 This information will go into row 1 column 2
This information will go into row 2 column 1 This information will go into row 2 column 2

The table that has just been coded doesn't have a border.
Most tables are easier to read if they have a border, so let's
add one to our table:

```
<table border="1">
    <tr>
        <td>This information will go into row 1 column 1</td>
        <td>This information will go into row 1 column 2</td>
    </tr>
    <tr>
        <td>This information will go into row 2 column 1</td>
        <td>This information will go into row 2 column 2</td>
    </tr>
</table>
```

The table now looks like this:

| This information will go into row 1 column 1 | This information will go into row 1 column 2 |
| This information will go into row 2 column 1 | This information will go into row 2 column 2 |

You can also format your border when you code your table:

```
<table style="border:5px dotted green">
```

This will put a dotted green border around the outside of your table.

```
<td style="border:1px solid green">This information
will go into row 1 column 1</td>
```

This will put a solid green border around the first cell.

This information will go into row 1 column 1	This information will go into row 1 column 2
This information will go into row 2 column 1	This information will go into row 2 column 2

Or you can add the styles to the document header:

```
<style>
     body
     h1   {font-family:sans-serif; font-size:32pt;}
     h2   {font-family:sans-serif;font-size:24pt;
     table {border:5px dotted green; border-collapse:collapse;}
     td {border:1px solid green;}
</style>
```

> This gives you a border with a single line rather than a double line.

Plan-IT

7.3.2 Plan, using a wireframe, a table to add to your web page showing key dates in your computing hero's life.

Compute-IT

7.3.3 Code the table you planned for 7.3.2 Plan-IT into your web page.

Embedding content from other websites

It is possible to embed content from other websites, such as video clips and audio clips, in your web page. A good way to do this is to insert an **iframe**. Most websites will give you the code that you need to copy and paste into your web page. It normally begins with `<iframe>` and ends with `</iframe>`. Remember what you learnt in Unit 6 about plagiarism? Don't forget to reference any content you use from another website, so the viewer knows where it came from originally.

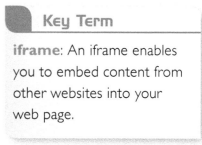

Key Term

iframe: An iframe enables you to embed content from other websites into your web page.

▲ Websites such as YouTube are very popular, because people can upload videos and embed them in their own web pages. Click on 'Share' and then on 'Embed', and cut and paste the code into the code for your web page.

Think-IT

7.3.4 Look at the screenshot from YouTube above.

   a) What does `width="560" height="315"` mean?

   b) What does `frameborder="0"` mean? What would happen if you changed the 0 to another number?

7.3.5 a) How do you think the web browser will display the embedded content if the code reads `<iframe width="100%" height="100%">`?

   b) What do you think will happen when you change the size of the web browser application window?

Compute-IT

7.3.6 a) Find a video clip or a sound clip about your computing hero and embed it into your web page.

b) Now alter the properties of the embedded content and test the predictions you made in 7.3.5 Think-IT.

Challenge

Your challenge for this unit was to code a web page and upload it to a server. Now that you have coded your web page, it is time to upload it.

Compute-IT

7.3.7 When you upload your web page you will need to give it a filename. When a web browser is directed to a website and the URL does not contain a filename, the browser will usually look for the default file.

The name of this default file will be specified by the server on which the web page is hosted. It is often `index.html` or `index.htm`, but the server administrator can set it to anything they like. Alternative names include `welcome.html` or `welcome.htm`, or `default.html` or `default.htm`. Most web browsers and web servers handle HTM and HTML extensions in the same way.

Which you use is usually up to you; however, if you want to make your web page the default page for the website, you will need to find the name that has been given to the default file on the server and match it exactly.

A final thought:

HTML is not the only markup language. Markup languages are everywhere, and have been a part of computing since the birth of the personal computer. For example, word processing uses a compressed markup document, with files for pictures, called Open Document Text or ODT.

Think-IT

7.3.8 Why do you think that open formats are important for storing data?

Designing for HCI: a hand-held digital device

Challenge

Your challenge is to design, for a specific user group and using future technology, a hand-held digital device to include phone functionality.

8.1 HCI and changing technology

What is Human–Computer Interaction (HCI)?

Human–Computer Interaction (**HCI**) is the study of how people (users) interact with computers. It is important not to let the word 'computer' limit your vision of HCI to a person sitting at a desk in front of a computer. HCI also refers to things like getting cash from an ATM, checking the instrument panels on an aeroplane, monitoring control systems in manufacturing plants, observing scientific experiments and composing music using both hardware and software.

Some technologies have changed dramatically over the last few decades, and the pace of change is speeding up. The way humans and computers interact has changed the way we work and the way we live our lives.

WIMP

The introduction of **WIMP** (Windows, Icons, Menus and Pointer) in 1980 is often cited as one of the great leaps forward in computing. Until WIMP was introduced, users controlled computers via the command line. In WIMP systems:

W the 'windows' give computers the opportunity to run multiple programs at the same time, each in their own window

I an 'icon' acts as a shortcut to execute the program

M a 'menu' is used to aid selection – it might be text- or icon-based

P a 'pointer' is represented as a symbol on the screen and its movement is controlled by a physical device.

Key Term

Human–Computer Interaction (HCI): HCI is the study of how people (users) interact with computers.

Think-IT

8.1.1 List as many words as you can think of when you see the term 'Human–Computer Interaction'.

Key Term

WIMP: A way of implementing a graphical user interface. WIMP stands for Windows, Icons, Menus and Pointer.

▲ The BBC Micro, with no WIMP (left), and Apple's Macintosh 1984, with WIMP (right)

WIMP interaction was popularised when Apple introduced the Macintosh in 1984. Apple also added the concept of the 'menu bar'.

More recently, there have been advances in **touchscreen** technology. A touchscreen is a visual display that enables the user to interact directly with the elements in the display with single or multiple finger touches. Although it is not such a significant leap forward as the introduction of WIMP, touchscreen technology has changed the way that humans interact with computers and they can be found on a range of digital devices, such as tablet computers. User interfaces designed for touchscreen computers are often seen as more difficult to use than older technology.

> **Key Term**
>
> **Touchscreen**: A visual display that enables the user to control a device through single or multiple finger touches to the screen.

Think-IT

8.1.2 Why might ease of use be affected when software that has been designed for one type of interaction – for example, touchscreen or WIMP – is used on a device with older or newer technology?

Think-IT

8.1.3 List the common devices that feature touchscreens.

HCI has become a very important part of the design process for the development of all software and hardware, and there are lots of jobs for HCI experts in many industries, from gaming to biomedical engineering.

The development of mobile phones

The first mobile phone call was made in 1973 and, as you can see from the timeline, mobile phones have been commercially available for a few decades. The very first commercial mobile phone call was made on 13 October 1983, when Bob Barnett, president of the telecommunications company Ameritech, placed a call from Chicago to the great grandson of Alexander Graham Bell in Germany.

▲ A timeline showing the development of the mobile phone

Think-IT

8.1.4 a) List changes in mobile phone design that have taken place since the first commercial mobile phone call in 1983. Think about the size, weight and shape of the devices, and the method of interaction, not just the screen elements.

b) What is the motivating force behind these changes, both good and bad?

c) Why do you think the interfaces and hardware design for hand-held digital devices are similar?

Think-IT

8.1.5 The first commercial mobile phones were controlled by key presses. Now many are controlled by direct gestures and voice recognition. What will mobile phones be like in 20 years' time? What new technologies will have developed by then and what impact might these changes have on the user? Think about your different senses:

■ Vision: What will mobile phones look like? How will they be used by sighted people and people with visual impairments?
■ Hearing: What will mobile phones sound like? Will they work better in a noisy environment? How will they be used by people with a hearing impairment?
■ Touch: What will mobile phones feel like? How will people interact with them using touch? How will they be used by people with physical disabilities or young children who haven't yet developed fine motor skills?

Designing with a specific user in mind

Designers should always keep in mind the people who are going to use their products or services. **Personas** have been used in IT development since the late 1990s to help with this.

A persona is not a specific person or a perfect example of the person who will be using a design. It is a way of applying a set of characteristics to a user group. Developing the profile of a 'typical' user (i.e. giving them a name, a face, a background story and anything else of relevance) helps the designer focus on the product's user and use.

Key Terms

Persona: A profile of a typical user, which is used as a tool throughout the design process to ensure the user is kept in mind at all times.

App: An **app**lication is typically, a small and specialised computer program that can be downloaded onto a mobile device.

Rachel

Age: 35

Occupation: Works in the accounts department of a small manufacturing firm and looks after two children, Jake aged 15 and Rosa aged 12. Her husband James works away a lot.

Likes: Being very organised and knowing where everything is and what everyone is doing.

Dislikes: A messy, cluttered house and no food in the kitchen cupboards.

What is a typical day like? Rachel gets up early and prepares breakfast for her family. She makes sure Jake and Rosa have everything they need for school, although she tries not to boss them too much because they are old enough to organise themselves now. She then gets the bus to work, where she is busy all day. She tries to get out to the supermaket at lunchtime to buy food for the evening meal, but often doesn't get the chance so is always scrabbling around to make a tasty healthy meal from what she has in the cupboard when she gets home.
She tries to go for a swim at least once a week, to keep fit, but evenings are usually spent cooking and tidying and watching television with her family.

What daily challenges do they face? It's hard to juggle work and family and stay sane and organised; Rachel never seems to have any food in her cupboards.

What do they use a mobile phone for now? Rachel uses a mobile phone to stay in touch with her children via text and to call James when he is working away. She doesn't have a smartphone, as she isn't really sure what she would use all the extra functionality for.

What could they use a mobile phone for? A shopping app, which Rachel could use while she is on the bus, might help resolve one of the big stresses in her life. It would need to be simple to use, and Rachel would need to be confident that her debit card details were secure while she was using it.

▲ An example of a persona created to support the development of a shopping **app** for a busy working mum

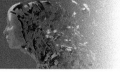

When you create a profile of a 'typical' user, you are creating a **stereotype** (from the Greek words for 'solid and firm' and 'impression'), which, if used in the right way, can be useful to designers.

Plan-IT

8.1.6   Remember that your challenge is to design a hand-held digital device for a specific user group. Choose one of the user groups below and create a persona for it:

a) An elderly person over the age of 70.

b) A young child aged 7.

Talking to your user group

A persona is a useful tool that helps you consider how a user group thinks and feels, but there is no substitute for talking directly to members of a user group. Often the data you collect from interviews helps you to think about a problem in a different way, providing you with insights into the way something is done that you would never have thought of yourself. This fresh understanding can then influence the persona you create.

To make the most of the data collection opportunity, it is important to prepare a questionnaire before you interview people from your user group. Questionnaires can contain two different types of questions:

Closed questions

These are structured questions with a defined answer, which gather data about the frequency of viewpoints and events. For example:

1. Do you own a hand-held digital device?   Yes ☐   No ☐

2. On a scale of 1 to 5, how easy do you find using your current hand-held digital device, with 1 being 'not at all easy' and 5 being 'very easy'?   1   2   3   4   5

Use a scale of 1 to 5 when you are asking what your interviewee thinks about something. It helps them clearly articulate their thoughts.

It is possible to record data collected from closed questions and analyse them in a spreadsheet.

Open questions

These are unstructured questions, which uncover information about feelings and behaviour. Open questions can often be more useful than structured questions when thinking about usability and accessibility. For example:

1. Why don't you have a handheld digital device?

....

....

2. What problems do you have using a hand-held digital device at the moment?

....

....

3. If you have a learning or physical disability, how does it affect how you use a hand-held digital device?

....

....

The data collected from open questions can be analysed by summarising the feelings and behaviour it has shown you.

Plan-IT

8.1.7 Prepare a questionnaire for your user group.

a) Begin by thinking about what you want to know; the things that will help you design the perfect hand-held digital device for your user group. Did any questions emerge when you were creating your persona?

b) Next, for each thing you want to know, decide whether an open question or a closed question would be most likely to produce a useful answer.

c) Write your questionnaire.

d) Ask someone to look at your questionnaire and give feedback. Are there any changes you want to make as a result of their feedback?

e) Decide how many people you are going to interview, thinking about how many responses you will need to ensure the results are valid.

Compute-IT

8.1.8 Carry out your interviews and analyse the data you collect.

8.2 Future technologies and prototyping

Researching future technologies

Some technologies develop and evolve more quickly than others. Many children in more economically developed countries have never known a world without laptops and hand-held digital devices, yet people over the age of 65 were born into a world where the very idea of carrying a phone around with you in your pocket was the stuff of science fiction. By way of a contrast, are cars really any different from the way they were 20 years ago?

▲ Near Field Communication (NFC) is an existing technology that enables devices to communicate with each other when they are brought close together. The NFC ring fuses this technology with a wearable device that can open your front door, start the car, pay for goods and much more.

▲ In 2013, Samsung told the world about its YOUM Flexible Display. If you're looking at this book in a few years' time, are flexible displays common or did the idea fail to take off?

▲ A Volkswagen Golf Mark 1 (above) introduced in 1974, and a Volkswagen Golf Mark 7 (below) released in 2013.

Plan-IT

8.2.1   Carry out some research to find out if any of the new technologies being developed or imagined today will help to solve some of the problems young children or elderly people have with mobile phones? Try using some of the web search skills you developed in Unit 6 to perform this task as efficiently as possible.

Designing a prototype

A **prototype** is a functional model of a design, which can be used to demonstrate (usually to the user) how a design works, and to check that it meets the design criteria. A prototype will usually go through several iterations before the final design for a product emerges.

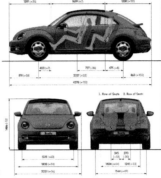

▲ Early designs for a new Volkswagen car

▲ A prototype in a wind tunnel

Compute-IT

8.2.2 Create a prototype of your hand-held digital device.

a) Start by sketching your design, annotating it with notes that explain how each feature meets the needs of your user group. Don't forget to refer to your research findings in your notes.

b) Build a model of your design.

Think-IT

8.2.3 Once you have completed your prototype, think back to the questionnaire you wrote for your user group. Was there anything you forgot to ask? If you refer back to the persona you created, will that help you answer these questions?

Think-IT

8.2.4 Look at the two images on the right.

The numbers on a keyboard number pad or a calculator are arranged differently from the numbers on a mobile phone. Do you think that the calculator layout performs better when the user is doing a lot of data entry and the mobile phone layout performs better when dialling a number? If yes, what are the criteria for 'better'?

8.3 Testing, evaluation and iteration

A prototype is made to be tested. The feedback provided by users during the test phase is then used to produce another iteration of the prototype, which fixes problems or introduces new features. That iteration is tested again, and another prototype is produced. And so the cycle of testing, evaluation and iteration goes on until the designer, or whoever they are working for, is happy with the product or has to get it to market because money is running short.

These are designs for a badge, which is awarded to people who create effective visualisations of data. The designer produced four iterations of the design before it was finalised.

> This is the first attempt. I realised I hadn't really thought about the purpose of the badge or who would be receiving it. I went for something I liked, which isn't really good design practice. I needed to think about the end user more.

The first iteration

> This is my second attempt. It tries to represent data visually, using blocks to symbolise a bar chart, to link with the purpose of the badge better. It doesn't feel like it's quite there yet, though.

The second iteration

> I really like the use of green and black to illustrate the command line interface in this design, and there is a real sense of the volume of data. I don't think the word 'Data' works by itself though, and I wonder if it looks a bit messy.

The third iteration

> In this final iteration I have pulled together all the things I liked from my previous versions – the text from the first iteration, the blocks to symbolise the bar chart from the second iteration and the use of colour from the third iteration – and I think it works. I think it is as near to perfect as any design will ever be.

The fourth and final iteration

Compute-IT

8.3.1 **a)** Test your prototype of your hand-held digital device. Ask the person doing the testing:
- What works well? Why?
- What would be even better if…? Why?

b) Evaluate the feedback from the person who tested your prototype and produce a second iteration of your prototype, remembering to keep the user group you are designing for in mind at all times. Describe the changes you have made and why you have made them.

Compute-IT

8.3.2 Test your second prototype, evaluate the feedback and produce another iteration of your hand-held digital device.

Challenge

Your challenge for this unit was to design a hand-held digital device for a specific user group, using future technology. You have:
- explored the development of the hand-held digital device
- researched the needs of your user group
- researched future technologies
- designed several iterations of your prototype.

Compute-IT

8.3.3 Prepare a presentation to pitch your hand-held digital device design to an investor who might finance its development. Remember to explain how each feature of the device meets the needs of the end user you designed it for.

Designing for HCI: an operating system interface

9.1 What is an operating system interface?

An **operating system** (or **OS**) is the software that manages a computer's basic functions, such as scheduling tasks, executing applications and controlling the devices connected to it (the 'peripherals', such as a printer or a mouse). Some operating systems that you might have seen or used are Microsoft Windows or Linux on a PC, OS X on an Apple Mac, iOS on an Apple iPhone or iPad, or Android on a smartphone.

The interface, or **user interface** (**UI**), is the part of the operating system that allows information to pass between the computer's operating system and the user in a way that the user can understand and interact with easily.

A computer employs several different UIs for different purposes and different users. The design of the interface should enable users to access programs, functions and facilities easily, using suitable input and output.

Some interfaces will be graphical. A **Graphical User Interface** (**GUI**) is an interface that uses graphics rather than text. WIMP (Windows, Icons, Menus and Pointer), is a GUI, but there are other GUIs that do not use WIMP, such as the GUIs of most smartphones and tablets.

Think-IT

9.1.1 List the operating systems that you are aware of. What do they have in common? For example, are their windows, icons, menus and pointers similar? And how do they differ?

Compute-IT

9.1.3 How has the design of interfaces for operating systems changed over the years?

Compute-IT

9.1.2 Investigate the accessibility features available on the operating systems you have access to. Consider their usability using the system usability scale (SUS).

The SUS is the industry standard questionnaire for measuring perceptions of usability. It is technology independent, and has even been used to measure the usability of telephone directories. To use the SUS, answer the following questions using a scale from 1 for 'strongly agree' to 5 for 'strongly disagree'.

1 I think that I would like to use this system frequently.

2 I found the system unnecessarily complex.

3 I thought the system was easy to use.

4 I think that I would need the support of a technical person to be able to use this system.

5 I found the various functions in this system were well integrated.

6 I thought there was too much inconsistency in this system.

7 I would imagine that most people would learn to use this system very quickly.

8 I found the system very cumbersome to use.

9 I felt very confident using the system.

10 I needed to learn a lot of things before I could get going with this system.

When you have answered all ten questions:

- Look at the odd-numbered questions, and subtract one from each response.
- Look at the even-numbered questions, and subtract each response from five.
- Add up the resulting numbers and multiply the total by 2.5.

An SUS above 68 is considered above average, while an SUS below 68 is considered below average.

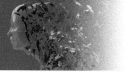

Command line interface (CLI)

The command line interface enables the user to give instructions to the computer directly, using single characters, whole words or abbreviations. It was the first active dialogue-style interface used with a computer and is still widely used in spite of the many menu-driven interfaces available today.

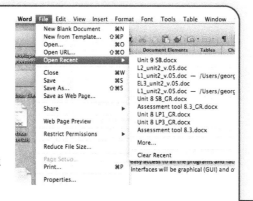

```
                        george2 — bash — 76×20
unset [-f] [-v] [name ...]          until COMMANDS; do COMMANDS; done
variables - Some variable names an wait [n]
while COMMANDS; do COMMANDS; done   { COMMANDS ; }
GEORGEs-iMac-2:~ george2$ history
    1  java
    2  brandy load cricket
    3  brandy load downloads/brandy/examples/cricket
    4  brandy load /Users/george2/Downloads/brandy-1.0.16/examples/cricket
    5  commands
    6  help
    7  /Users/george2/Downloads/brandy-1.0.16\ 2/README ; exit;
    8  cd '/Users/george2/Documents/Hodder Nats/Files 8.1.1/' && '/usr/bin/p
ythonw' '/Users/george2/Documents/Hodder Nats/Files 8.1.1/city.py'  && echo
 Exit status: $? && exit 1
    9  help
   10  clear
   11  dir
   12  help
   13  history
GEORGEs-iMac-2:~ george2$
```

Menu interfaces and forms interfaces

A menu interface uses toolbars and keyboard shortcuts to communicate with the operating system. Menu interfaces come in various different forms, including roll over, pop up, pull down or drop-down menus. The right click function on a mouse is an example of a menu interface.

A forms interface is often used when extra information, which must be supplied by the user, is required to complete the action. For example, when you click on 'Save as…' you are presented with a form that asks you to supply a filename and location for the file to be saved.

Different operating system interfaces

Head-up display (HUD)

A head-up display is the name given to any transparent display that presents data without requiring users to look away from their usual viewpoints. The origin of the name stems from a pilot's need to be able to view information with their head up and looking forwards, instead of angled down looking at lower instruments. Although they were initially developed for military aviation, HUDs are now used in commercial aircraft, automobiles, and other applications.

WIMP interfaces

The screenshot shows several windows. You can see different icons, each representing a different file type or program. Along the top there is a tool bar containing icons. Above this, there are pull-down menus where further commands are available. WIMPs are graphical user interfaces that use a mouse or a multi-touch surface to enable us to manipulate icons in order to carry out tasks.

Speech-recognition interfaces

Speech-recognition interfaces, which are also known as voice-recognition interfaces, allow people to issue commands and dictate tasks using their voice. Speech-recognition interfaces have existed for a while but many operating systems haven't taken advantage of the technology. Examples of voice recognition systems include Siri for the iPhone and vlingo for Xbox.

One of the difficulties with speech-recognition interfaces is that natural language is very difficult for computers to understand. It would be good to be able to communicate with a computer in natural language. It would mean that anyone could make a complex machine work without a lot of formal training. However, if you ask a Help menu, 'How do I print this document double-sided?' you are unlikely to get the correct answer first time, if at all. People make grammatical errors or are imprecise or verbose (using more words than they need to) when they speak, which can make it hard to interpret their wishes. Artificial language is often more concise and precise than natural language. 'Print double-sided how?' is more likely to get you the information you're after.

Touch- or gesture-control interfaces

One of the first touch- or gesture-control screens was the DiamondTouch table, which was developed by Mitsubishi Electric Research Laboratories (MERL) in 2001. Two or more people could sit at the table and interact with the screen, and the screen knew which person was doing what.

Press and hold for more information

Tap for main action

Slide to pan across

Pinch or stretch to zoom in or out

Turn to rotate

Swipe from edge for app or system commands

Now touch- or gesture-control interfaces are used in smartphones and tablets. The signal travels from the touch point to the processor as electrical impulses. The processor analyses the data it receives, noting for example where the touch starts and ends. It then sends the instructions to the operating system to carry out the required tasks. And it all happens in a matter of nanoseconds.

9.2 Designing an operating system interface

What does your user want?

Just as it is important to keep your end user in mind when you are designing hardware, it is also important to keep them in mind when you are designing software. For example, if a mobile phone handset has been carefully designed for an elderly person to use, with an easy-to-grip casing, it makes good commercial sense to ensure that the operating system is also easy for an elderly person to use and that the phone does exactly what they need it to do. The same goes for a phone designed for a young child. Users with fewer skills will require more guidance, for example.

Think-IT

9.2.1 Find the persona and questionnaire you created for Unit 8, as well as the data you collected from your user group and the final prototype for your hand-held digital device. Use the information to answer the following questions:

a) What problems do your users have interacting with the operating system on their hand-held digital device?

b) How might the interface be redesigned to resolve some or all of the problems they are experiencing?

Plan-IT

9.2.2 Once you know how the user will be interacting with your hand-held digital device, you need to consider what they will be doing with the device. You need to identify what the user's objectives are and what features your device will provide to meet those objectives. You then need to describe how easy your features will be for your target audience to use. Do this by copying and completing the first three columns in the table below.

User's objectives	Features	Usability	Evaluation

9.2.3 Gather feedback on your ideas, asking the person providing the feedback to complete the 'Evaluation' column in your table.

9.2.4 Will any of the new technologies being developed or even imagined today help you to better meet some or all of your user's objectives? Search the web for information about new technologies and look again at 9.2.1 Think-IT and 9.2.2 Plan-IT.

Producing a wireframe

A **wireframe** is a visual guide showing how the features of a piece of software function, how the different aspects of a design link together. For example, it might show you what a mobile phone screen will look like before a particular button is pressed and what it should look like after the button is pressed.

Key Term

Wireframe: A visual guide showing how the features of a piece of software function, how the different aspects of a design link together.

▲ A wireframe of a revision app for smartphones

Compute-IT

9.2.5 Create a wireframe showing how the operating system interface for your hand-held digital device will be structured and how the user will navigate through it.

Don't forget that, when designing your operating system interface, you should always be asking yourself the following questions:

- WHAT will the user interface (UI) look like?
- HOW will it work?
- WHY is this a benefit to the end user?

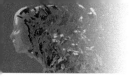
9.3 Testing, evaluation and iteration

Key Term

Iteration: Using repetition of a process to create a more efficient solution.

A wireframe is designed to be tested just like a prototype, so the feedback provided by users during the test phase is used to produce another **iteration** of the wireframe, which fixes problems or introduces new features. That iteration is tested again, and another wireframe is produced. And the cycle of testing, evaluation and iteration goes on until the designer, or whoever they are working for, is happy with the product or has to get it into the market because money is running short.

You used iteration when you designed algorithms in Unit 3 and when you designed your hand-held digital device in Unit 8.

Observational research and task analysis

In Unit 8, you used a questionnaire to gather information from your user group. Questionnaires are very useful when you know what you want to ask, but are less useful when you want to find out how someone responds to something. This is because people aren't always able to describe accurately their thoughts, feelings and responses. Sometimes it is simply better to observe a person doing something and then use your observations to further develop your design.

When carrying out observational research it is important to explain clearly to the person you're observing exactly what you want them to do. For example, before you observe a young child using a wireframe for a mobile phone operating system interface you will need to explain briefly how the wireframe works. You will need to tell them that they turn to a different image every time they 'press' a button, 'swipe' the screen or issue a voice command. Ask them to think aloud while they're working, and ask them afterwards how it went.

▲ Observational research in action

If they seem lost or confused at any point you will want to ask them why and what they are thinking, because perhaps your design is unclear. Their feedback will help you improve it.

Observational research can be used to perform **task analysis**. Task analysis is the name given to the process of closely studying the way people perform HCI tasks. Every aspect of a specific task – including how frequently it is performed, how long it takes, how complicated it is, what the user's emotional response to completing it is, when it is completed, the equipment needed to complete it, as well as other things that will be specific to the task itself – is monitored and recorded.

> **Key Term**
>
> **Task analysis**: The name given to the process of closely studying the way people perform HCI tasks.

Compute-IT

9.3.1 a) Test your wireframe for your hand-held digital device's interface by carrying out task analysis. Ask the user to do something that you identified your interface will do in 9.2.2 Plan-IT and watch them completing the task using your wireframe.

b) Evaluate the feedback you received from your research and produce a second iteration of your wireframe, remembering to keep the user group you are designing for in mind at all times. Describe the changes you have made and why you have made them.

9.3.2 Test your second wireframe, evaluate the feedback and produce another iteration of your hand-held digital device's operating system interface.

Challenge

Your challenge for this unit was to design an operating system interface for the hand-held digital device you designed in Unit 8, thinking about the technology that will be available in the future and about the needs of your specific user group.

You have:

- explored different operating system interfaces
- considered the needs of your user group
- researched future technologies
- designed several iterations of your wireframe.

Compute-IT

9.3.3 Prepare a presentation to pitch your operating system interface for your hand-held digital device to an investor who might finance its development. Remember to explain how each feature of the device meets the needs of the end user you designed it for.

Challenge

Your challenge is to learn about static images so you can stream a video.

10.1 Pixels and pixelated images

Pixels and pixelated images

Tiny squares, called **pixels**, are the building blocks of all digital images on your computer, tablet or mobile phone screen. The word 'pixel' is short for 'picture element' and each pixel is a small element on the screen that can be used to show colours.

The use of pixels can be traced back as far as the Romans. Although they did not have electronic screens, they used a very similar approach when making mosaics. Small pieces of coloured tile were placed in such a way that, when viewed from afar, you see the whole image rather than the individual elements.

The first-ever digital image is widely considered to have been created by Russell A. Kirsch in 1957. The picture consisted of 30 976 pixels and it was a scanned image of his baby son.

> **Key Term**
>
> **Pixel:** The smallest element on a screen. Image files on a computer are composed of many pixels.

▲ When you zoom in on an image on an electronic display, the more noticeable the pixels of an image become. This is similar to taking a close look at a Roman mosaic.

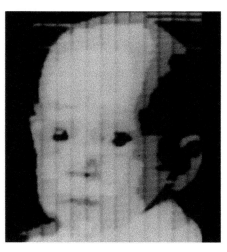

▲ This is considered to be the first-ever digital image, scanned by Russell A. Kirsch in 1957.

The image on the right is 1,200 pixels wide and 858 pixels high (1,200 × 858). The image looks sharp and clear.

Below is a section of the same image, but zoomed in 500%. You will notice the image does not look as clear. The image starts to lose its realistic, smooth appearance and starts to look 'blocky'.

The third image is zoomed in 1,600% and you can quite clearly see the pixels appearing in the picture, just like the tiles on a Roman mosaic. When an image looks 'blocky' like this, we say it is **pixelated**.

▲ The original image

▲ Zoomed in 500%

▲ Zoomed in 1600%

Early computer games used to feature very pixelated graphics.

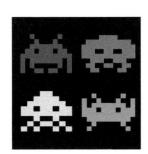

Key Term

Pixelated: This is the term used to describe an image when the individual pixels are clearly visible.

One-bit image representation

Pixels are the elements used to build images on an electronic screen, but the computer needs to know how to colour the pixel to produce the image. As with all information stored on a computer, this information is stored in binary.

The amount of binary code used to store the information depends on the number of colours you want to use in the picture. A one-bit image requires one bit of binary for each pixel in the image. As one bit of binary only gives us the choice of two numbers, 0 or 1, an image with one bit can have just two colours. These colours tend to be black (1) and white (0) but don't have to be.

The binary for the image below (left) is:
000000000000000011000000000100100000001000010000010
100101000100011000100100011000100010100101000001000010
000000100100000000001100000

It is easier to view the binary code in a table below (right).

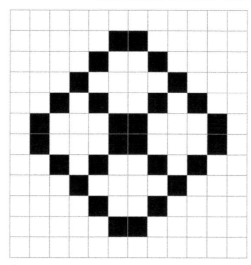

▲ A one-bit image

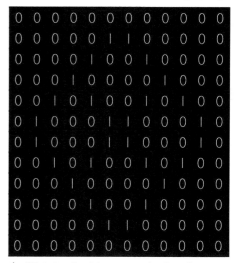

▲ This is the binary code for the image on the left.

Compute-IT

10.1.1　**a)** Using the binary data below, create a one-bit retro gaming character using spreadsheet software or online pixel art software. The gaming character should be black and white.

001000000100000100010000011111111000110110110111111111111110111111101101000001010 001101100000000000000000000000000000000000000

Before you begin you will need to think about how many rows and columns the grid that contains the binary data for the gaming character will be. HINT: It's a square!

b) Create your own one-bit pixel image and write down its binary string. Then pass your code to another student to see if they can recreate your image.

Colour depth

As you increase the number of bits per pixel (bpp), the number of colours you can use increases. The term 'colour depth' is used to describe the number of bits used to indicate the colour of a single pixel. For example:

One-bit image	2^1 = 2 colours	0, 1
Two-bit image	2^2 = 4 colours	00, 01, 10, 11
Three-bit image	2^3 = 8 colours	000, 001, 010, 011, 100, 101, 110, 111

Images with higher colour depth use more bits per pixel and this affects the size of the image file. As the colour depth gets larger, so does the size of the file. The HDMI specification used on modern televisions uses up to 30-bit colour depths, which is equal to 1.073 billion colours. The human eye can, however, distinguish only around 10 million colours.

> **Key Term**
>
> **Colour depth**: The term used to describe the number of bits used to indicate the colour of a single pixel.

Think-IT

10.1.2 How many different colours will a four-bit image have? An eight-bit image? How about a 24-bit image?

Compute-IT

10.1.3 **a)** How many bits are needed for each of the following colour depths? 256, 64, 32, 16, 8 and 4 colours.

b) Using a suitable eight-bit (256 colour) BMP image, reduce the colour depth of the image to 64, 32, 16, 8 and then 4, remembering to save from the original file and maintain the same image format each time. Compare the actual file size with the expected number of bits.

c) Compare the quality of the image for each colour depth. What happens every time the colour depth is reduced?

Think-IT

10.1.4 What is the largest digital photo ever taken?

▲ The same image in 24, 8 and 4 bit colour depth

10.2 Image size and file types

Resolution

You need to consider both the **resolution** of the screen you are using and the resolution of the image or video you are watching.

For images and video, the resolution is simply the number of pixels that makes up the content. It is normally given as the number of pixels horizontally followed by the number of pixels vertically, for example, 1024 × 768. The more pixels that make up the image or video, the higher the resolution and the clearer it will look to the human eye.

A screen also consists of pixels. Early displays had fewer pixels than today's. The early Nokia phones, for example, had a screen made up of 84 × 48 pixels, whereas the iPhone 5s has a screen made up of 1136 × 640 pixels. The new 4K televisions have a resolution of 3840 × 2160.

▲ A Nokia 3310 with a resolution of 84 × 48 and an iPhone 5s with retina display

It isn't simply the case that the higher the resolution of a screen, the better the quality of the image, because the size of the screen itself is also a factor. A lower resolution on a small display might look just as good as a higher resolution on a larger display. Compare watching a YouTube video with your smartphone held close to your face with watching the same clip on a much larger screen at a distance. Quality depends on the **pixel density**. For example, Apple's '**retina display**' is not a fixed resolution. It just means that the display has at least 300 pixels per inch of screen. The first iPad with a retina display needed a resolution of 2048 × 1536 to have 300 pixels per inch on a 9.7-inch screen. In contrast, the MacBook Pro needs a resolution of 2880 × 1800 to achieve the same effect on its larger 13-inch screen.

> ### Key Terms
>
> **Pixel density**: The number of pixels per inch of the display.
>
> **Retina display**: A screen on which individual pixels cannot be distinguished by the human eye when it is at least 10.5 inches away. This is calculated to be at least 300 pixels per inch of screen.

Think-IT

10.2.1 Find the screen resolution and pixel density of your mobile phone's display.

When viewing images or video on a display, the size and quality of the content will differ depending on the display it is being viewed on. An image with a resolution of 120 × 120 will look very tiny on a screen with a resolution of 1680 × 1050, and if you were to zoom in to fit the image to the screen size, it would look very pixelated. Ideally, the content you are viewing should match the screen resolution of the device you are watching it on to get the best image quality.

Think-IT

10.2.2 View a video on YouTube that has been uploaded with a 1080p (high definition) option.

Lower the quality to the lowest possible setting. Watch the clip on normal view and then expand it to full screen. Do you notice a difference in quality?

Load another tab with the same video, set one version to 1080p and the other to 720p. Can you tell the difference in quality between the two on the normal view? How about when they are expanded to full screen?

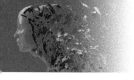
Bitmap images: An image made up of a grid of pixels.

Vector images: An image made up of lines, curves and shapes, which are drawn using mathematical calculations.

Image types

Images are produced on a screen using one of two different methods: **bitmap images** are made up of pixels on a grid, whereas **vector images** use lines, curves and shapes that are calculated mathematically to create the image.

Bitmap images

Bitmaps, sometimes known as raster images, are the type of image you looked at when learning about colour depth and screen resolution. They are made up of a number of pixels in a grid system, and they suffer from pixelation when they are made larger than their original resolution.

There are a number of different bitmap formats. JPEG ('j-peg'), BMP ('bitmap'), GIF ('jiff') and PNG ('ping') are the most widely used and have different capabilities and limitations.

The file size of this photograph is ▶ 35.3 MB in its raw state. The 'File size' column in the table below shows what happens to the file size when the photograph is saved in different formats.

'Lossy' means that there is some loss in the quality of the image when it is compressed.

Name	Colour depth supported	Transparency	Animation	Compression	File size	Common uses
JPEG	24-bits per pixel	No	No	Yes (lossy)	Very small 1.19 MB	Large photos on web pages
GIF	8-bits per pixel	Yes	Yes	Yes (lossless)	Small 7.86 MB	Animations or logo-style graphics
PNG	Up to 48-bits per pixel	Yes	No	Yes (lossless)	Small 9.94 MB	Small photos on web pages
BMP	Up to 64-bits per pixel	No	No	No	Large 35.4 MB	Photos kept on a computer

'Lossless' means that there is no loss in the quality of the image when it is compressed.

Some of the formats use **compression**. This allows you to make the image size smaller than the original. However, when an image is compressed some data is lost and this can affect the quality of the image, especially if it is heavily compressed. JPEG images suffer from this the most, but the advantage is that a heavily compressed image will be a lot smaller than the original so it will load faster and the image will display more quickly on a web page.

> **Key Term**
>
> **Compression:** The process of reducing the bit-size of a data file by removing unnecessary information.

Compute-IT

10.2.3 a) Find two PNG images, like the ones on the right. One should be an artwork with a transparent background and one a photograph.

b) Using a suitable program, save both images as JPEG and GIF files.

c) Use the information about the image to complete the following table for each image.

File type	Transparency	File size	Image quality
PNG			
JPEG			
GIF			

Vector images

Vector images are drawn to fit the screen using paths and control points. This means that the format contains the details of the lines, shapes and curves used in the image and the computer uses mathematical calculations to draw these to correspond accurately to the screen they are being viewed on.

The big advantage of using vector images is that they are scalable. This means the image can be resized and will not pixelate like a bitmap image does. Also, vector images do not have to be square or rectangular like bitmap images; they can be any shape.

There are limitations to using vector images, however. Complex images, such as photographs, are too complicated to produce as vector images because of the number of calculations needed to draw them to match a screen.

The standard file format for a vector image is a Scalable Vector Graphic (SVG).

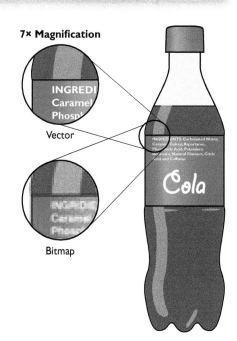

7× Magnification

Vector

Bitmap

▲ This shows the effect of resizing a vector image compared with resizing a bitmap image.

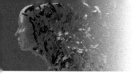

10.3 Steganography and moving images

Introducing steganography

Steganography is a Greek word that means 'concealed writing'. In Ancient Greece, many people exchanged messages by carving them into wax tablets. However, some people carved secret messages into wooden tablets, then melted wax onto them and carved another message into the wax. Most people saw only the wax carving, but those in the know could melt the wax to reveal the message carved into the wood. If you have ever used invisible ink to write a message on paper, which is only revealed when you scribble over it with another pen, then you have already used a form of steganography.

Another kind of steganography, which you may have come across, is the null cipher. This is a message that was sent by the German Embassy in Washington during the Second World War:

> PRESIDENT'S EMBARGO RULING SHOULD HAVE IMMEDIATE
> NOTICE. GRAVE SITUATION AFFECTING INTERNATIONAL
> LAW. STATEMENT FORESHADOWS RUIN OF MANY NEUTRALS.
> YELLOW JOURNALS UNIFYING NATIONAL EXCITEMENT
> IMMENSELY.

It seems innocent enough to anybody who reads it, but to the intended recipient, who knows to take the first letter from each word to form a message, it means something else entirely.

> PERSHINGSAILSFROMNYJUNEI

Or PERSHING SAILS FROM NY JUNE I

Nowadays, most steganography is carried out digitally. This means people use techniques and algorithms to hide messages or other data in digital files. These files can be anything from image or music files to files hidden in the system folders of operating systems. The secret message can be particularly difficult to detect, because, to the unsuspecting eye, the digital file looks and behaves exactly as expected. There is no indication it contains any hidden data.

> **Key Term**
>
> **Steganography:** The art of hiding a message in such a way that only the people writing and receiving the message know that it is there.

Take this image for example.

It is a photograph of Bletchley Park. It looks like a normal photo, and even if you zoomed in very close to look at individual pixels, you would not notice anything unusual. However, inside the binary data that makes up the photo there is a hidden message.

This message can be inserted into the image by adding extra bits to the file (described below) or by using the Least Significant Bit (LSB) method (page 127).

Adding extra bits to the file

This method works by adding the data you want to hide to the file. The photograph of Bletchley Park contains thousands of bits of data, but let us assume that the binary data below describes the whole image.

```
0  0  1  1  1  0  0  1
0  1  1  1  1  0  1  0
1  1  1  0  0  0  1  1
1  0  1  0  1  1  0  1
1  0  0  0  1  1  1  1
0  0  0  1  1  0  1  0
1  1  1  1  0  0  1  1
1  1  0  1  1
```

If you want to add the data 010 into the file, it is likely to cause **data corruption** if you just inserted it into the middle of the code. The way the photograph looks might be altered as a result, giving away a clue that a message might be hidden in the file, as you can see at the top of the next page.

Think-IT

10.3.1 Have you ever sent a secret message to somebody? How did you do it and did you get caught?

> ### Key Term
>
> **Data corruption**: An error in computer data that causes a file to be read or displayed incorrectly.

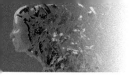

This is how the Bletchley Park photograph might look if 010 is added to the file. It is corrupted. Compare this image to the one on page 125.

Compare this image to the one on page 125.

> **Key Term**
>
> **Metadata**: Data about data.

However, all files contain a file header at the start of the file. This tells the computer what type of file it is and how to handle it. This data about the data is called **metadata**. Metadata would be a good place to store the data containing the secret message because it won't affect the actual look of the image. Similarly, storing the secret message data at the end, after the end of file data, would also not affect the image.

The secret message data has been inserted after the end of file data.

```
0  0  1  1  1  0  0  1
0  1  1  1  1  0  1  0
1  1  1  0  0  0  1  1
1  0  1  0  1  1  0  1
1  0  0  0  1  1  1  1
0  0  0  1  1  0  1  0
1  1  1  1  0  0  1  1
1  1  0  1  1  0  1  0
```

The downside to this method is that adding data to a file causes the file size to increase. Someone seeing an image with an extremely large file size might become suspicious, because they know an image would not normally be that large, and might guess that it contains hidden data.

Least Significant Bit (LSB)

Another method of hiding data is called Least Significant Bit or LSB. This method, rather than adding extra bits to the data, changes or replaces data within the file.

Take, for example, a photograph with 24-bit colour depth. This means that each pixel is coloured using 24 bits of data.

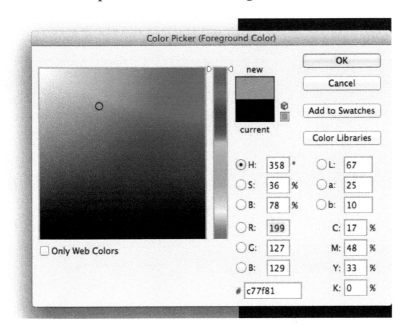

The binary data for this pixel is 110110101001011010010101 or, viewed in an easier way:

Red	= 11011010
Green	= 10010110
Blue	= 10010101

Using the LSB technique, you would alter the last bit of each byte, the least significant bit, so the above data would become:

Red	= 11011011
Green	= 10010111
Blue	= 10010100

This change to the data would be so small that it would be impossible to detect with the human eye.

Look at the image on the right. The eight-bit colour on the left is not the same as the eight-bit colour on the right – it is one bit different. Can you see the difference?

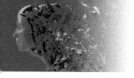

Key Term

Steganalysis: The name given to the process of discovering messages hidden using steganography.

With a 24-bit colour, the change is even less noticeable, and the advantage to the LSB method is that the file size stays the same, making it very hard to identify that an image contains a secret message.

When you consider that the data inserted into the file might be encrypted too, it makes **steganalysis** highly complex, and makes steganography an important skill for those who want to communicate secretly.

Compute-IT

10.3.2 H. L. Dennis, the author of *Secret Breakers: The Power of Three*, has hidden the location of the Golden Phoenix on her website using steganography.

Go to **http://hldennis.com/birthdaymessage** and download the image. Then zoom in on it to spot the hidden message, which, when added to the end of **http://hldennis.com/** will form another web address (**http://hldennis.com/************).

Go to this web page to continue your journey to identify the location of the Golden Phoenix.

HAVE A TREMENDOUS TIME

AND ENJOY SO MUCH THE

DELIGHT OF

A GREAT DAY

Wishing you a very
Happy Birthday

HAPPY 10 TH

BIRTHDAY

BRODIE MAY

Moving images

You now understand how static images are displayed, but what about moving images, videos and animations? In fact, there is little difference between static images and moving pictures. Videos and animations are simply lots of static images that are rapidly displayed one after another giving an illusion of movement.

Challenge

Compute-IT

10.3.3 It is time for you to complete the challenge for this unit. You know all about static images and how they are displayed on a digital display, and it is now time for you to stream video like a computer by creating a paper flipbook. Each page of your flipbook represents a single image file made up of millions of bits of data.

A paper flipbook can be made by cutting up a lot of squares of paper and stapling them together into a small book. You draw the first image on the last sheet of paper and change the image slightly on each following sheet of paper until you have drawn a complete sequence of images in the book from back to front. By flipping through the book from the last page to the first page you will be able to 'stream your video'.

Be creative and see how many images you can create in the time available. Then show your completed flipbook to your neighbour.

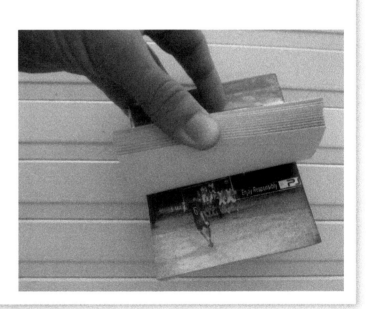

Think-IT

10.3.4 A video is streamed in the same way as a flipbook, as a sequence of static images. The refresh rate is the number of images that are displayed per second. What effect would a slow refresh rate have on the quality of a video?

Think-IT

10.3.5 High-definition (HD) video uses a fast refresh rate and high-resolution images. What effect will this have on the size of HD video files?

10.3.6 Why do video files take much longer to download from the internet than text and static image files?

Challenge

Children in a primary school have asked you to program a simple shape calculator, using a graphical programming language of your choice such as Scratch, to help them with their maths. They have sent you a page from their Maths textbook to give you an idea of the type of calculations they need help with.

Quick revision

1 Complete these calculations.
   a) 490 + 219 =
   b) 93 − 37 =
   c) 24 × 8 =
   d) 54 ÷ 6 =

2 Calculate the perimeter of this square.

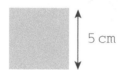

5 cm

3 Calculate the perimeter of this equilateral triangle.

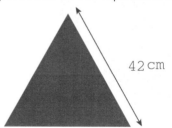

42 cm

4 Calculate the area of this shape

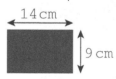

14 cm

9 cm

Key Term

Operation: Any action performed by a computer, such as performing a calculation or processing data in other ways.

Think-IT

11.1.1 Look at the page from the maths textbook you have been provided with. What mathematical **operations** does the calculator need to be able to run?

11.1 Programming variables

Analysing calculations

Before you can program the calculator you need to analyse the calculations to find out exactly what is going on and what the calculator will need to do.

23 + 89 = 112

This can be represented in algebra as:

$$a + b = c$$

> a, b and c are variables. This means that the numerical values of a, b and c can change but the description of the calculation as a whole will still be accurate.

In your calculator program you are going to assign a value to the answer **variable**, in this case c. You write this calculation as:

$$c = a + b$$

To assign a value to c, you must first know the values of a and b, so the process is:

1 Enter the value for a.
2 Enter the value for b.
3 Set c to $a + b$.

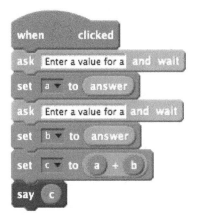

If you subtract a from both sides, you can also write $c = a + b$ as $c - a = b$. To assign a value to b you must first know what values a and c have so the process is:

1 Enter the value for c.
2 Enter the value for a.
3 Set b to $c - a$.

Key Term

Variable: A named location in memory used to store data.

Think-IT

11.1.2 **a)** Note that the order of each variable is important when subtracting numbers. Is the order important when you multiply (*) and divide (/) numbers?

b) Which variables are inputs? In a calculator program, who or what does the inputting?

c) Which variables are outputs? In a calculator program, who or what does the outputting?

HINT: Think back to your work in Unit 1 in which you learned all about what goes on under the hood of a computer.

Programming variables

When a user inputs data into a computer, the computer stores it and retrieves it from a named place in the memory called a variable (see Unit 5). Being able to use variables is a key computational thinking skill because they help you to write programs that employ abstraction and generalisation. If you use a variable to represent an important element of your program, the value of that element can change without you needing to rewrite the program to make the change happen.

It is good practice to choose names for variables that indicate what they are. For example, if you use the names 'height' and 'width' for the sides of a shape it is easy to work out which side of the shape the variable refers to. This is very useful when trying to find errors in programs, especially in large programs.

If you call the three variables in 23 + 89 = 112 `num1`, `num2` and `total`, respectively, and you input the following for the first two variables:

```
num 1    num2
23       89
```

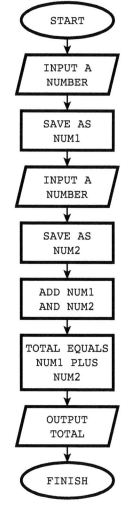

the computer will look up what is stored in each of the memory locations, add them together and output:

```
total
112
```

Flowcharts

A **flowchart** is a diagram that represents a series of events using shapes linked by arrows. Ovals are usually used to start and finish flowcharts. Inputs and outputs are represented by rhomboids. Rectangles are used for operations. Arrows denote the flow. Flowcharts are very useful for planning out how to program a computer.

A flowchart for the calculation you have been working on is shown on the left.

 Key Term

Flowchart: A diagram that represents a series of events using shapes linked by arrows.

Plan-IT

11.1.3 Using flowcharts or structured English, explain the process involved in programming a computer to calculate the area of a 9 cm by 8 cm rectangle.

11.1.4 The blocks used in graphical programming languages are often colour coded to indicate their purpose. Colour code the instructions you created for 11.1.3 Plan-IT, using the key provided with the graphical programming language you are using, to indicate which blocks you will use to program each event.

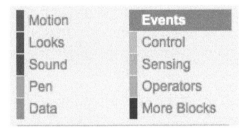

▲ This is the key provided with Scratch 2.0.

Compute-IT

11.1.5 Create a simple calculator using a graphical programming language of your choice. Use only one sprite and interface with the user using input blocks.

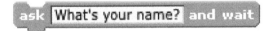

▲ In Scratch 2.0, the input blocks are called 'ask' blocks.

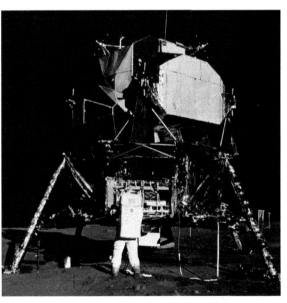

▲ The calculator on the left has 32× the processing power of the Apollo Guidance Computer, that landed the Apollo 11 Lunar Module on the Moon.

◀ A modern-day graphical calculator will perform many more functions than your program, but at a basic level the code will be similar.

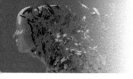

11.2 Programming operations

Challenge

The primary school pupils like what you have created so far, but they need to use separate programs for each maths operation, and this is slowing down their work, so the challenge is to redesign the simple calculator to allow the user to choose which operation is used to perform the calculation.

Making choices

Where a choice has to be made in a computer program, it is important to identify the paths that will be followed as a result of each **selection** that is made.

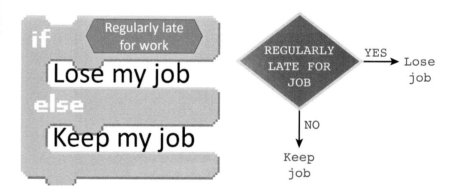

If the condition at the top of the block next to 'if' is met, then the top path will be taken. If the condition is not met then the bottom 'else' path will be followed. In this type of selection only one choice or the other choice can be carried out.

Think-IT

11.2.1   What other 'if else' selections can you think of, and what would their real-life consequences be?

Decision diamonds and selection

A decision diamond is used in a flowchart to represent selection.
A standard decision diamond always has two choices: 'yes' or
'no'. For example:

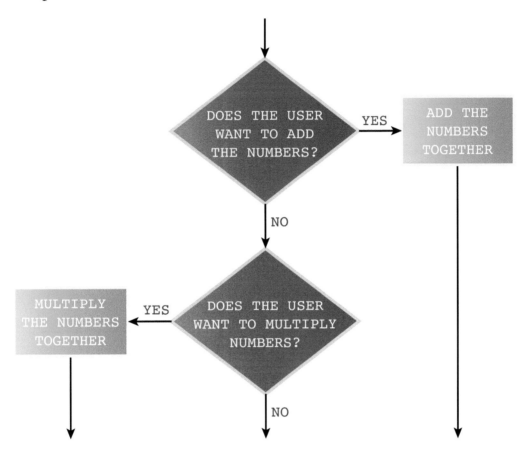

Computer scientists have adapted this flowchart shape so that
it can more easily represent modern multiple choices like this:

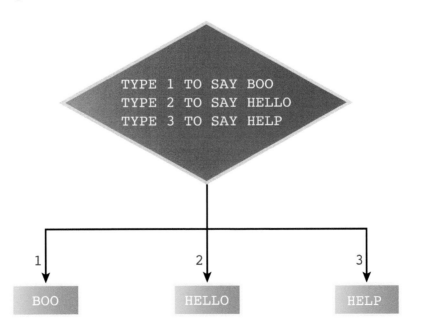

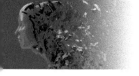

You can use a multiple 'if' selection. Every 'if' selection checks to see if the answer is equal to its condition. If the condition is met then the code will be run. In Scratch it would look like this:

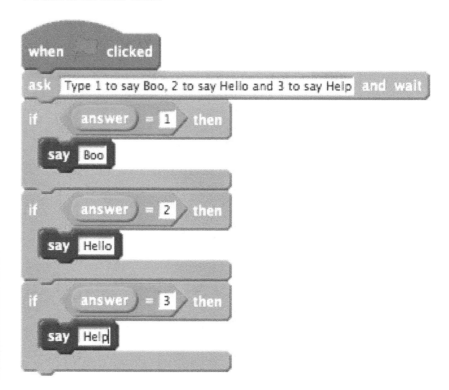

Think-IT

11.2.2 Is there a problem with the multiple 'if' approach described above?

Plan-IT

11.2.3 Plan a calculator program in which the user can choose which maths operation (+, −, * or /) to use.

Key Term

Debug: The process of correcting code to fix mistakes.

Compute-IT

11.2.4 Use your plan to create a calculator program that uses selection, in a graphical programming language of your choice. Don't forget to test and **debug** small parts of your code as you create it.

Mistakes (bugs) are a common part of programming. Finding errors and fixing them is a real skill. Try to work out what part of your program is causing the problem. If a classmate or your teacher has working code, compare yours with theirs and try and spot the difference. Try reading the code out loud to see if it makes sense in the context of what you are trying to achieve. Get a classmate to work with you; sometimes you can't see your own mistakes. Or try running your code one block at a time to see if that isolates the problem.

Commenting code

Programming is often carried out collaboratively, so it is important to have a method of communicating with the other people working on the project. **Commenting code** is the name given to the process of leaving notes in the code to remind yourself or help others understand why things have been done in a particular way.

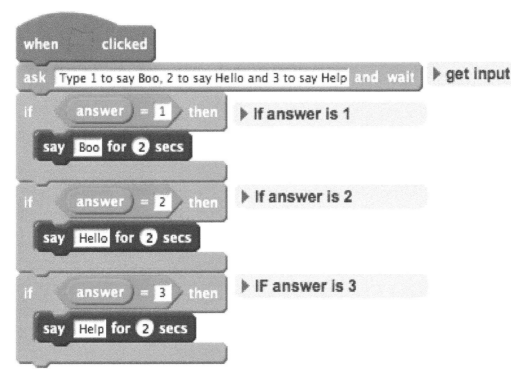

▲ In Scratch 2.0, you can add comments to the program by right-clicking in the script area, but away from the script itself, and then selecting 'add comment'.

Compute-IT

11.2.5   Comment the code you created for 11.2.4 Compute-IT.

11.3 Using procedures and functions

Challenge

A parent of one of the primary school pupils who has been using your calculator works for a large software developer. They like your calculator but need it to use procedures if they are to mass-produce it as most programming languages use procedures or functions.

Key Terms

Procedure: A procedure is a sequence of programme instructions that have been abstracted and can be used over the over again. It can accept input from other parts of the program.

Function: Like a procedure, a function is a sequence of program instructions that have been abstracted and can be used over and over again. Again, like a procedure, it can accept input from other parts of the program, but it can also return information to other parts of the program.

Procedures and functions

Procedures and **functions** are sub-programs. They are sections of code that can be used over and over again. Both can accept inputs, which are also called parameters, from other parts of the program, but a function can also return information to other parts of the program.

Let's look at an example of a program that draws squares with sides of different lengths and calculates their perimeter using a function.

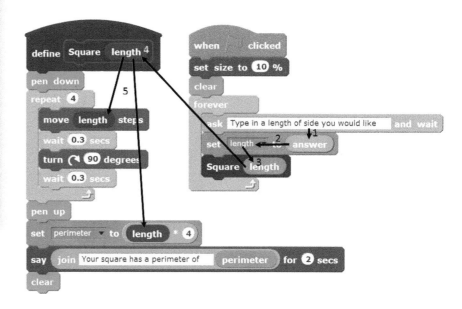

The user is asked to input the length of the side (1). Their answer is then placed inside a variable called 'length' (2). 'length' is then passed to the function called 'square' (4) and is used to move the sprite and calculate the perimeter (5). Here the function is within a forever loop so it is used over and over again.

Think-IT

11.3.1 If a user typed in 25 into the square drawing program (at the bottom of page 138) what would the printed perimeter be? How could the code for the program that draws a square and calculates the perimeter be adapted to calculate the area of a square? What about a rectangle?

Challenge

It's now time to finalise your shape calculator to help primary school pupils with their maths.

Think back to the work you did in Unit 3 about drawing shapes. Can you reuse those ideas here to help you create your shape calculator?

▲ This is a part of a Scratch 2.0 program. It draws a square.

Plan-IT

11.3.2 Plan a way to rework the calculator program you wrote in 11.2.4 Compute-IT to use procedures and functions. This means making the calculator you created previously capable of calculating perimeters and areas, so that it can perform all the calculations contained in the maths book the primary school pupils gave you at the beginning of the lesson.

Compute-IT

11.3.3 Program your shape calculator using a graphical programming language.

11.3.4 Can you adapt your program to make it more appealing to younger pupils? What about adding some animation or sound to your program?

Challenge

The challenge for this unit is to program a maths quiz for primary school pupils. The quiz should ask the player for their name, and then use this in the questions. The quiz should contain sections of questions, each covering a different maths topic. At least one section should contain questions that the computer has generated randomly. All the answers should be numerical.

12.1 Abstraction

What is abstraction?

Welcome to my quiz about computing.

Please write down your name.

What is the name of the first computing programming language?

The answer is 'ADA'. Give yourself one point if you got this right.

Who was the first computing programming language named after?

The answer is Ada, Countess of Lovelace. Give yourself one point if you got this right.

What was the name of the machine that the first computing programming language was written for?

The answer is the analytic machine. Give yourself one point if you got this right.

Please give me your final scores.

There are a number of steps involved in a quiz like the one shown in the cartoon:

1 The Quiz Master (QM) welcomes the Quiz Takers (QTs) to the quiz.
2 The QM asks the QTs to write down their name.
3 The QM asks the QTs a question.
4 The QTs answer the question.
5 The QM provides the correct answer and tells the QTs how many points they receive if they got the answer right.
6 Steps 3, 4 and 5 are repeated until all the questions have been asked.
7 The QM asks for the final scores.
8 The QTs provide their final scores.

Thinking about the quiz abstractly, by removing the detail of the questions and their answers, helps you to focus on what is actually happening. **Abstraction** is an important skill for computer scientists. It enables you to consider other ways to do things. For example, the quiz could also be run like this:

1 The Quiz Master (QM) welcomes the Quiz Takers (QTs) to the quiz.
2 The QM asks the QTs their names.
3 The QM asks a question.
4 The QTs answer the question.
5 Steps 3 and 4 are repeated until all the questions have been asked.
6 The QM provides the correct answers and tells the QTs how many points they receive for each correct answer.
7 The QM asks the QTs for their final scores.
8 The QTs provide their final scores.

> **Key Term**
>
> **Abstraction**: Working with ideas or solving a problem by identifying common patterns in real situations, concentrating on general ideas and not on the detail of the problem itself.

Think-IT

12.1.1 What other common processes in the steps above could you abstract by removing specific detail?

Using abstraction to help with the challenge

Abstraction will help you to complete the challenge.

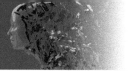

Plan-IT

12.1.2 Copy and complete the following table, matching each step in an abstract quiz with one or more blocks from a graphical programming language.

Step in abstract quiz	Instruction from a graphical programming language
The QM welcomes the Quiz Takers (QTs) to the quiz.	
The QM asks the QTs their names.	
The QM asks a question.	
The QTs answer the question.	
The QM provides the correct answer.	
The QM tells the QTs how many points they receive if they got the answer right.	

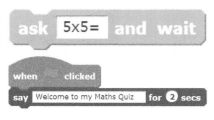

▲ These are the Scratch 2.0 blocks that you could use.

Understanding how a quiz question is programmed in Scratch 2.0

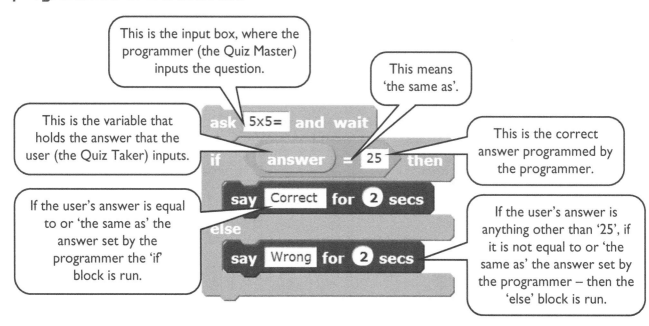

This is the input box, where the programmer (the Quiz Master) inputs the question.

This means 'the same as'.

This is the variable that holds the answer that the user (the Quiz Taker) inputs.

This is the correct answer programmed by the programmer.

If the user's answer is equal to or 'the same as' the answer set by the programmer the 'if' block is run.

If the user's answer is anything other than '25', if it is not equal to or 'the same as' the answer set by the programmer – then the 'else' block is run.

Plan-IT

12.1.3 Design an algorithm for a quiz with a series of maths questions.

Compute-IT

12.1.4 Program the quiz you wrote an algorithm for in 12.1.3 Plan-IT.

Compute-IT

12.1.5 Raj and Maria have created this code in Scratch 2.0, including a 'Score' variable in their quiz. Unfortunately it is not working as they thought it would. Can you debug their code?

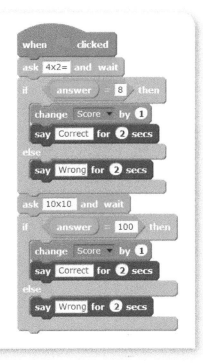

Variables

As you know from Unit 11, when a user inputs data into a computer, the computer stores it and retrieves it from a named place in the memory called a **variable**.

The programmer can decide whether the variables will be constant or changeable, depending on what the program needs. In our maths quiz, you can therefore decide to generate automatically the numbers that make up the questions by calling the first variable num1 and the second variable num2 and randomly generating a new value for each variable on each loop. The variable called total will change on each loop as num1 and num2 are added together and the answer is placed inside it.

> **Key Term**
>
> **Variable**: A named location in memory used to store data.

Think-IT

12.1.6 Raj and Maria's Scratch program, which you can see in 12.1.5 Compute-IT, shows how the variable, the score, is used within that program. Work your way through the code and ask yourself if it will work. If it does work, will it work every single time the program runs? Is there a bug that needs to be fixed? If so, how would you fix it?

Plan-IT

12.1.7 Using what you have learned so far about abstracting quizzes and creating and scoring quiz questions, and what you learned programming a calculator in Unit 11, design a quiz where the numbers that make up the questions are randomly generated by the computer, as a flow diagram or using structured English.

12.2 Decomposition and generalisation

What is decomposition?

In computer science, 'decomposition' is the name given to the process of breaking a problem or a program down into smaller and more manageable chunks. Computer scientists do this so that they can concentrate on finding a solution to a specific part of a problem without worrying about all of it in one go. It is also a useful tool for programmers because most programs are created by teams of people and if the program is decomposed, using procedures and functions, then different members of the team can work on different parts of the program at the same time.

Using decomposition to help with the challenge

Decomposing a quiz will provide ideas for the challenge.

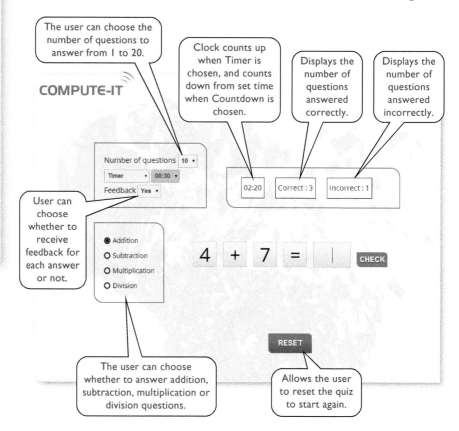

Key Terms

Decomposition: The process of breaking something down into smaller parts.

Procedure: A procedure is a sequence of program instructions that have been abstracted and can be used over the over again. It can accept input from other parts of the program.

Function: Like a procedure, a function is a sequence of program instructions that have been abstracted and can be used over and over again. Again, like a procedure, it can accept input from other parts of the program, but it can also return information back to other parts of the program.

Random number generators

A random number generator generates a sequence of numbers, characters or symbols that appear to lack a pattern and seem to be random. Random number generators can be computational and physical. Physical random number generators have been used since ancient times.

Think-IT

12.2.1 List as many physical random generators you can think of. HINT: Think about your maths lessons.

12.2.2 Where are computational random number generators used today?

There are ways to measure randomness, using statistics, which require large amounts of data. A sequence of numbers, characters or symbols is said to be statistically random when it contains no recognisable patterns or regularities. However, just because a sequence is statistically random doesn't mean it is truly random. Computational random number generators create sequences that appear to have no pattern, but often have repeated patterns over a very long sequence.

The required 'quality' of the randomness, the level of unpredictability, of an algorithm for generating random numbers depends on its use. For example, the randomness required in cryptography (protecting information by transforming it into a cipher that is unreadable) is very high. However, algorithms that generate questions for a quiz, and algorithms for searching or sorting, require only a low level of unpredictability.

Compute-IT

12.2.3 Program a quiz where the computer randomly generates the numbers that make up the questions.

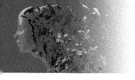

Key Term

Generalisation: Taking concepts used in the solution of a particular problem and using them to solve other problems that have similar features.

What is generalisation?

One of the beauties of computer science is replacing the many with the one. **Generalisation** replaces multiple blocks of code that do a similar job with one function or procedure that uses variables to provide the differences.

If you want to write a program for building houses, you would first decide on the features that define a house, such as foundations, external doors, floors, windows and rooms. Generalising, you can then write a program that includes these features as variables so you can identify the number of times these things occur in the house.

Features that define a house	Bungalow	Semi-detached house	Mansion
Foundations	1	1	1
External doors	2	2	4
Floors	1	2	3
Windows	6	8	12
Rooms	4	6	12

House 1 2 1 6 4 is a bungalow, House 1 2 2 8 6 is a semi-detached house and House 1 4 3 12 12 is a mansion.

Generalisation has helped computer scientists automate many factories. Before designing a robotic arm all the jobs that it will need to do are analysed.

▲ Robotic arms in a factory

The robotic arm is then designed to be able to reach far enough to do all of these jobs and flexible enough to have many different arms attached to it so it can carry them out. Workers at the factory will then program each robot to spray or rivet or screw.

Using generalisation to help with the challenge

Your addition quiz can be changed to a multiplication, subtraction or division quiz by adapting two blocks. You can use blocks that you have already designed and make small modifications to make them perform other tasks. This is generalisation: taking concepts used in the solution of one problem and using them to solve other problems that have similar features.

▲ In this Scratch 2.0 example, the addition blocks have been repeated and adapted to add subtraction questions to this quiz.

Think-IT

12.2.4 Look at the Scratch 2.0 example above. What happens if the random number generated for the variable num1 is smaller than the random number generated for the variable num2?

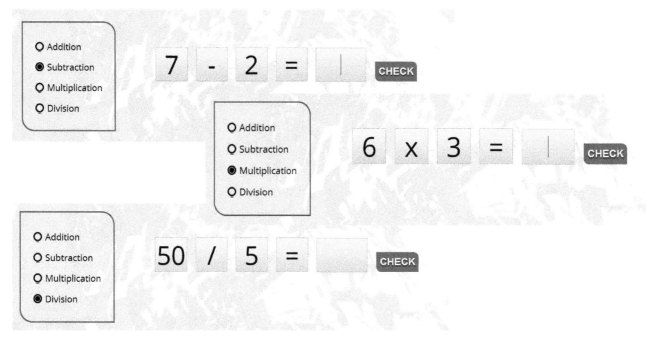

▲ This quiz allows users to choose to take subtraction, multiplication and division questions as well as addition.

Compute-IT

12.2.5 Create blocks for the other operations so that your quiz includes multiplication, subtraction and division questions as well as addition questions. Remember to think about the range of values you will generate for each of the operations.

Plan-IT

12.2.6 Plan how the quiz blocks will be organised. The image on the previous page shows them organised in sequence, but you might wish to organise them differently. You could

- allow the user to choose the order
- get the computer to choose the order randomly
- get the computer to choose the next set questions based on the quiz taker's score.

For the third method, for example, **if** the quiz taker scored more than eight for the addition questions then they move to the multiplication questions. Otherwise (**else**) they move to the subtraction questions.

Compute-IT

12.2.7 Modify your quiz program to include the blocks you created for 12.2.5 Compute-IT using the method of organisation you planned in 12.2.6 Plan-IT.

Targeting specific user groups

Think-IT

12.2.8 Units 8 and 9 were all about Human–Computer Interaction and designing computer hardware and software for a specific user group. You learnt about creating personas, profiles of typical users which can be used throughout the design process to ensure the user is kept in mind at all times. The challenge for this unit is to create a maths quiz for primary school pupils. How would you amend the quiz you have programmed to appeal to your specified user group?

▲ Will a brightly coloured, humorous quiz appeal to your user group?

Compute-IT

12.2.9 Amend the program you have created to ensure it appeals to your specified user group.

Don't despair if you are struggling. Incomplete attempts to complete a task are still very valuable. If you are unable to complete this activity, document your efforts using comments.

12.3 Adding a timer

Adding a timer to a quiz can provide an extra sense of excitement and challenge or it can distract the quiz taker or undermine their confidence. The effect of a timer depends on how it has been designed and the user group that will be playing the quiz.

▲ A countdown clock counts backwards to indicate the time remaining before an event, such as the end of the quiz, is scheduled to occur.

▲ A countup timer counts forwards to indicate how long something takes.

Countdown timers can be used to fix the time available to answer one question or to complete a whole quiz. The computer knows how long a second is because it uses a built-in clock to manage the CPU, which was discussed in Unit 1.

Countup timers can be used to tell the quiz taker how long it took them to answer each question or to complete the whole quiz. The time taken can then be subtracted from the quiz taker's score.

Think-IT

12.3.1 What sort of timer is most appropriate for your quiz program and your user group of primary school pupils?

Plan-IT

12.3.2 Design a timer for your quiz program using a flowchart or structured English.

Compute-IT

12.3.3 Program a timer for your quiz program.

Challenge

At the beginning of this unit, you were set the challenge of programming a maths quiz for primary school pupils. The quiz had to ask the player for their name and then use this in the questions. It had to contain sections of questions, each covering a different maths topic. At least one section had to contain questions that the computer generated randomly. All the answers had to be numerical.

By completing all the activities in this unit, you should have a program. Now it is time to finish it off.

Compute-IT

12.3.4 Test and **debug** your program. Mistakes, or 'bugs', are a common part of programming, but finding the errors and fixing them is a real skill. To help you debug, you could:

- compare your code with code you already know works correctly try to spot differences
- read the code out loud to see if it makes sense in the context of what you are trying to achieve
- work with a partner and use paired programming to help you uncover the problem – it is often hard to see your own mistakes
- run your code one block at a time to see if this isolates the problem.

Key Term

Debug: The process of correcting code to fix mistakes.

Compute-IT

12.3.5 Before you release your program to your user group you need to evaluate it. The quiz takers will want a program that:

- appeals to them and that they will want to play more than once
- loads swiftly and allows them to proceed with the quiz quickly
- has easy-to-follow instructions or is so simple to use that it doesn't need any instructions (something very few programs manage)
- does what they expect it to do and what it says it will do
- doesn't crash.

Finally, and perhaps most importantly of all, does your quiz meet the brief?

Does your quiz fulfil these requirements? If not, what can you do to change it so that it does?

Compute-IT

12.3.6 Create a short advertisement for your game, using clips to illustrate the mathematical functions it includes, its visual appeal and how easy and enjoyable it is to use.

Glossary / Index

Key term	Definition	Pages
Abstraction	Working with ideas or solving a problem by identifying common patterns in real situations, concentrating on general ideas and not on the detail of the problem itself.	22, 30, 89, 141
Accessibility	Accessibility is all about making sure that all users, including those with disabilities, can use the web page.	83
Accumulator	The name given to the place where the computer does all its calculations. Note instructions such as INP and PUT automatically refer to the accumulator so the operand does not need to be specified.	62
Algorithm	A set of step-by-step instructions which, when followed, solve a problem.	16, 34, 42
App	An application – typically, a small and specialised computer program that can be downloaded onto a mobile device.	101
Artefact	A man-made object, which is of educational, cultural or historical interest. Not all digital resources are man-made, and so are not true artefacts.	66
Assembly language	A programming language that uses easy-to-remember codes rather than binary to give a CPU an instruction. Mnemonic codes are used to represent operators and labels are used to represent operands. A mnemonic is a pattern of characters used to make something easier to remember.	61
Binary	A number system which uses two digits, 0 and 1. All electronic computation is carried out using the binary system. The binary number system is also called base 2.	9
Bit	The term 'bit' is used to describe one binary digit and is derived from BInary digiT.	12
Bitmap images	An image made up of a grid of pixels.	122
Boolean operators	For example, the connective words AND, OR and NOT. In the context of searching the web, they manage the results returned.	79
Byte	A string of bits (usually eight, for example 10010101) is called a byte.	12
Cascading Style Sheets (CSS)	Cascading style sheets are used to format the layout of web pages. Styles can be applied to whole websites and web pages, or to individual elements, making things simpler. Any styles applied directly to individual elements will override styles applied to the whole document.	90
Central processing unit (CPU)	The part of the computer that interprets and executes instructions.	6
Client	A computer connected to a network (possibly the internet) that can request data and process services made available by a server.	66
Colour depth	The term used to describe the number of bits used to indicate the colour of a single pixel.	119
Commenting code	The name given to the process of leaving notes in the code that remind yourself or help others why things have been done in a particular way.	137
Compression	The process of reducing the bit-size of a data file by removing unnecessary information.	123

Computational thinking	Thinking logically about problems (and the world) in terms of the processes involved, the data available, and the steps that need to be followed in order to achieve the desired goal.	*18*
Compute	The verb 'to compute' means to carry out mathematical calculations. Today, with electronic computers everywhere, the term is more commonly defined as 'the use of computers to solve problems'.	*2*
Coordinates	A set of values used to show an exact position. In two dimensions we use x and y values, where x is the distance across the page and y the distance up the page.	*34*
Data	A collection of facts without context, such as values or measurements.	*2, 18*
Data corruption	An error in computer data that causes a file to be read or displayed incorrectly.	*125*
Debug	The process of correcting code to fix mistakes.	*136, 151*
Decimal	The system that is normally used for counting and computation. It uses ten digits: 0, 1, 2, 3, 4, 5, 6, 7, 8 and 9. The decimal number system is also called base 10.	*9*
Decompose	Break a problem down into a series of simpler problems, which you can easily understand. The process of decomposing a problem is known as 'decomposition'.	*14*
Decomposition	The process of breaking something down into smaller parts.	*33, 144*
Dry run	To run through a program on paper to see how it works. A dry run records the state of each variable when each line of the program is executed, so it has one line for each line of code in the program.	*42, 63*
Execute	To carry out something, usually a set of instructions.	*43*
Flowchart	A diagram that represents a series of events using shapes linked by arrows.	*132*
Function	Like a procedure, a function is a sequence of program instructions that have been abstracted and can be used over and over again. Again, like a procedure, it can accept input from other parts of the program, but it can also return information back to other parts of the program.	*47, 138, 144*
Generalisation	Taking concepts used in the solution of a particular problem and using them to solve other problems that have similar features.	*22, 30, 89, 146*
Geometrical shapes	Shapes that are defined by a set of mathematical rules.	*32*
Grammar	A set of rules that define the relationships between words in a language.	*91*
Graphical programming	a programming language that allows users to create programs using graphics rather than text	*37*
Graphical User Interface (GUI)	An interface that uses graphics rather than text. A GUI can be WIMP but doesn't have to be.	*108*
High-level programming language	A programming language which is more abstracted, so easier to read and write and therefore more user-friendly.	*58*
Human–Computer Interaction (HCI)	HCI is the study of how people (users) interact with computers.	*98*
HyperText Markup Language (HTML)	HTML is the main markup language for creating web pages and displaying other information in a web browser. Hyper is from the Greek for 'over' and means that hypertext is more than just text. It is used to reference other text or documents.	*68, 82*
Hypothesis testing	A proposed explanation for something. You can test it, to see if it is correct, using scientific observation and investigation.	*20*

iframe	An iframe enables you to embed content from other websites into your web page.	96
Information	Information is data that has been processed by adding a meaning through interpretation and by asking questions. For example, the data 1 5 7 23 46 47 and 49 become information when you know that they are lottery numbers. Data may also have different meanings in different contexts; 111 is one hundred and eleven in decimal, seven in binary, or could be interpreted as three letter Is (three in Roman numerals).	18
Input device	An input device enables the user to 'input' data into a computer.	5
Internet	The internet is a global network of millions of connected computers.	66
Iteration	Using repetition of a process to create a more efficient solution.	35, 46, 105, 114
Memory	This is where a computer keeps the data that has been input, as well as software applications and the results of any processing it has carried out, for the short term. This memory is lost when the computer is off.	5
Metadata	Data about data.	126
Model	Something created to imitate a real-life situation.	20
Network	A group of inter-connected computers and the communication infrastructure that allows digital data and services to be shared electronically.	67
Operand	The part of a machine instruction that tells the CPU the data or memory location where the instruction – the operator – should be carried out.	61
Operating system (OS)	The software that manages a computer's basic functions, such as scheduling tasks, executing applications and controlling peripherals.	108
Operation	Any action performed by a computer, such as performing a calculation or processing data in other ways.	130
Operator	The part of a machine instruction that gives the CPU an instruction to do something.	61
Output device	An output device enables the user to receive information from a computer.	5
Pattern identification	Looking for identifiable patterns in raw data using data analysis.	20
Persona	A profile of a typical user, which is used as a tool throughout the design process to ensure the user is kept in mind at all times.	101
Pixel	The smallest element on a screen. Image files on a computer are composed of many pixels.	116
Pixel density	The number of pixels per inch of the display.	121
Pixelated	This is the term used to describe an image when the individual pixels are clearly visible.	117
Procedural abstraction	Hiding the detail of a process in a named procedure or function.	47
Procedure	A procedure is a sequence of program instructions that have been abstracted and can be used over the over again. It can accept input from other parts of the program.	47, 138, 144
Processor	The part of a computer that processes data according to the instructions it has been given. It provides the user with information.	5
Protocol	A standard set of rules and instructions to be followed by a computer.	70
Prototype	A functional model of a product, which is used to test and demonstrate its design.	105
Resolution	The number of pixels that make up a screen, vertically and horizontally.	120

Retina display	A screen on which individual pixels cannot be distinguished by the human eye when it is at least 10.5 inches away. This is calculated to be at least 300 pixels per inch of screen.	121
Search engine	A computer program that searches web pages for the search terms entered by the user and provides a list of the pages in which they appear.	78
Selection	The choice of which route to take through a computer program.	50, 134
Sequence	A sequence of instructions is a set instructions that must be followed one after the other in a specific order.	46
Server	A computer connected to a network (possibly the internet) that manages requests to access its digital services and data.	66
Steganalysis	The name given to the process of discovering messages hidden using steganography.	128
Steganography	The art of hiding a message in such a way that only the people writing and receiving the message know that it is there.	124
Stereotype	A widely held and simplified image or idea of a particular type of person or group of people. A stereotype might or might not be accurate when applied to an individual.	102
Storage device	This is where a computer stores files that have been created, as well as software that has been installed, for the longer term.	5
Syntax	The grammatical arrangement of words in a language, showing how they connect and relate to each other.	91
Task analysis	The name given to the process of closely studying the way people perform HCI tasks.	115
Text-based programming	a programming language that requires the user to write code in the form of a sequence of text-based instructions into the computer to create a program.	39
Touchscreen	A visual display that enables the user to control a device through single or multiple finger touches to the screen.	99
Usability	The process of making a web page quick and easy to use.	83
User interface (UI)	The part of the operating system that allows information to pass between the operating system and the user.	108
Valid	sound, defensible and well grounded. 'Validation' is the name given to the process of checking that something is valid.	91
Variable	A named location in memory used to store data.	62, 131
Vector images	An image made up of lines, curves and shapes, which are drawn using mathematical calculations.	122
Verification	The process of checking that the grammar, syntax and vocabulary of code are correct.	91
Web browser	An application that can be used to display information stored digitally as web pages on computers on the world wide web. Google® Chrome and Microsoft® Internet Explorer® are examples of web browsers.	67
WIMP	A way of implementing a graphical user interface. WIMP stands for Windows, Icons, Menus and Pointer.	98
Wireframe	A visual guide showing how the features of a piece of software/a website function, and how the different aspects of a design link together.	85, 113
World wide web (WWW or the web)	A system of interlinked digital web pages that are located on the internet, and made available to the public.	68

Acknowledgements

The Publishers would like to thank the following for permission to reproduce copyright material:

Photo credits:

All robot images used in Challenge boxes © julien tromeur – Fotolia.com.

All Scratch blocks © Scratch (http://scratch.mit.edu/), used with kind permission.

p.2 *l* © SSPL via Getty Images, *r* © Science Museum / Science & Society Picture Library -- All rights reserved.; **p.3** *tl* © Ben2 / Wikipedia Commons (http://commons.wikimedia.org/wiki/Commons:GNU_Free_Documentation_License_1.2), *tr* © Jean-Jacques Cordier – Fotolia.com, *bl* © okinawakasawa – Fotolia.com, *br* © Science Museum / Science & Society Picture Library -- All rights reserved.; **p.4** *keyboard* © verkoka – Fotolia.com, *mouse* © AG-PHOTO – Fotolia.com, *hard disk drive* © sorapop – Fotolia.com, *CPU* © indigolotos – Thinkstock.com, *RAM* © luminaparis – Fotolia.com, *power supply* © Coprid – Fotolia.com, *fan unit* © Denis Dryashkin – Fotolia.com, *motherboard* © Jonathan Zander (Digon3) / Wikipedia Commons (http://commons.wikimedia.org/wiki/Commons:GNU_Free_Documentation_License_1.2), *monitor* © Evgeny Karandaev – Thinkstock.com, *headphones* © japolia – Fotolia.com, *microphone* © picsfive – Fotolia.com, *webcam* © Volodymyr Krasyuk – Fotolia.com, *sound card* © Jaroslavs Filsh – Fotolia.com, *graphics card* © Jenny Thompson – Fotolia.com, *desktop system* © believeinme33 – Fotolia.com, *Raspberry Pi* Image taken by Steve Connolly, reproduced by kind permission of Raspberry Pi; **p.6** © David J. Green - technology / Alamy; **p.8** *l* © SSPL via Getty Images, *r* © Matt Crypto – Wikipedia Commons (http://en.wikipedia.org/wiki/File:Lorenz-SZ42-2.jpg); **p.14** © Syda Productions – Fotolia.com; **p.16** © UIG via Getty Images; **p.17** © djama – Fotolia.com; **p.19** Courtesy of Wikipedia Commons (http://en.wikipedia.org/wiki/File:Snow-cholera-map-1.jpg); **p.20** *l* © NATIONAL LIBRARY OF MEDICINE/SCIENCE PHOTO LIBRARY, *r* © Justinc / Wikipedia Commons (http://en.wikipedia.org/wiki/File:John_Snow_memorial_and_pub.jpg); **p.21** © The Science Picture Company / Alamy; **p.25** © Pascal Deloche/Godong/Corbis; **p.28** © David Leahy / Digital Vision / Getty Images; **p.29** *l* © Robert Kerr / Alamy, *r* © Photimageon / Alamy; **p.31** *tl* © Dennis Hallinan / Alamy, *tr* © Classic Image / Alamy, *bl* © REUTERS/Olympic Delivery Authority, *br* © REUTERS/Olympic Delivery Authority; **p.32** *tl* © Sharpshot – Fotolia.com, *tr* © Abigail Woodman, *bl* © Smileus – Fotolia.com, *br* © igor - Fotolia.com; **p.33** © Peter Horree / Alamy; **p.36** © Arto – Fotolia.com; p. 37 *m* © Hopscotch Technologies, (gethopscotch.com), *r* © Alice Project, (www.alice.org); **p.38** *t* © dbimages / Alamy, *b* © Tom Grundy / Alamy; **p.39** *tl* © hollygraphic – Fotolia.com, *tr* © Robert Preston Photography / Alamy, *bl* © Python Software Foundation, *br* © Ruby / Yukihiro "Matz" Matsumoto; **p.43** *t* © REX/Tony Kyriacou, *b* © supergenijalac – Thinkstock.com; **p.50** © Jevtic – Thinkstock.com; **p.52** © underdogstudios – Fotolia.com; **p.54** © Ancient Art & Architecture Collection Ltd / Alamy; **p.55** *tr* © INTERFOTO / Alamy, *mr* © NEW YORK PUBLIC LIBRARY/SCIENCE PHOTO LIBRARY, *ml* © GeorgeOnline / Wikipedia Creative Commons Attribution Share-Alike 3.0 (http://creativecommons.org/licenses/by-sa/3.0/deed.en), *br* © Science Museum / Science & Society Picture Library -- All rights reserved.; **p.56** *t* © Getty Images, *m* © SSPL via Getty Images, *b* © http://history-computer.com/ - Wikipedia Creative Commons (http://en.wikipedia.org/wiki/File:Tommy_Flowers.jpg); **p.57** *t* © Corbis, *bl* © Science Museum / Science & Society Picture Library -- All rights reserved., *br* © Bettmann/CORBIS; **p.58** *t* © The National Museum of Computing, tnmoc.org, *mt* © VOLKER STEGER/SCIENCE PHOTO LIBRARY, *mb* © S. Kaba / Wikipedia Commons (http://en.wikipedia.org/wiki/File:74series_logic_ic.jpg), *b* © Konstantin Lanzet / Wikipedia Commons (http://en.wikipedia.org/wiki/File:KL_Intel_D8086.jpg); **p.59** © Yaca2671 / *Wikipedia Creative Commons (http://commons.wikimedia.org/wiki/Commons:GNU_Free_Documentation_License_1.2) Courtesy of Texas Instruments Incorporated*; **p.60** *tl* © The Granger Collection / TopFoto, *br* © John W. Mauchly Papers Kislak Center for Special Collections, Rare Books and Manuscripts University of Pennsylvania; **p.67** © The Opte Project – Wikipedia Commons (http://creativecommons.org/licenses/by/2.5/deed.en); **p.68** *l* Courtesy of Apple Inc., *m* © Mozilla Foundation and Mozilla Corporation, *r* © Google; **p.69** © FilmMagic / Getty Images; **p.70** © PAUL MILLER/epa/Corbis; **p.77** *tl* © Hemeroskopion – Fotolia.com, *mr* © olly – Fotolia.com, *b* © kids.4pictures – Fotolia.com; **p.80** *t* © birdeyefotolia – Fotolia.com, *m* © olgakr – Thinkstock, *b* © DAJ – Thinkstock.com; **p.87** *car crash* © kostasaletras – Fotolia.com, *explosion* © stefanholm – Fotolia.com, *aeroplane* © magann – Fotolia.com, *heart* © anastarass – Fotolia.com, *guitar* © seniorcarlo – Fotolia.com, *city* © Alan Reed – Fotolia.com; **p.89** © Getty Images; **p.99** *l* © REX/Jonathan Hordle, *r* © AP/AP/Press Association Images; **p.100** *from l to r* © REX, © Discostu / Wikipedia Commons (http://en.wikipedia.org/wiki/File:Nokia_3210_3.jpg), © Peter D Noyce / Alamy, Courtesy of Apple Inc., © Sergio Azenha / Alamy, © Robert Ramos / Demotix/Demotix/Press Association Images; **p.101** © duckman76 – Fotolia.com; **p.104** *tl* © Jae C. Hong/AP/Press Association Images, *tr* © NFCRing.com, *ml* © Volkswagen, *bl* © Volkswagen; **p.105** *all t* © Volkswagen, *bl* © leungchopan – Fotolia.com, *br* © Qyzz – Fotolia.com; **p.106** *all* © contrastwerkstatt – Fotolia.com; **p.101** © Coneyl Jay / Stone / Getty Images; **p.111** © JUNJI KUROKAWA/AP/Press Association Images; **p.114** *all* © Hodder Education; **p.116** *l* © Patrick Eden / Alamy, *r* Courtesy of Wikipedia Commons (http://en.wikipedia.org/wiki/File:NBSFirstScanImage.jpg); **p.117** *t & m* © Carl Turland, *b* © PiXXart Photography / Alamy; **p.119** *all* © George Rouse; **p.120** *l* © Nokia, *r* Courtesy of Apple Inc.; **p.122** © Lydia Young; **p.123** © davemhuntphoto – Fotolia.com; **p.125** Courtesy of Wikipedia Commons (http://en.wikipedia.org/wiki/File:Bletchley_Park.jpg); **p.126** Courtesy of Wikipedia Commons (http://en.wikipedia.org/wiki/File:Bletchley_Park.jpg) Adapted by Carl Turland; **p.129** © Josila / Creative Commons (http://creativecommons.org/licenses/by-sa/3.0/deed.en); **p.133** *l* © Lydia Young, *r* © NASA; **p.146** © Kuzihar – Thinkstock.com; **p.149** © Purestock – Thinkstock.com; **p.150** *l* © UncleSam – Fotolia.com, *r* © burnel11 – Fotolia.com.

t = top, b = bottom, l = left, r = right, m = middle

Every effort has been made to trace all copyright holders, but if any have been inadvertently overlooked the Publishers will be pleased to make the necessary arrangements at the first opportunity.